Guiding Kids Through the Tough Moments

Families, classrooms, all kinds of human groups are intricate, evolving social and emotional worlds. They exist to protect and nourish but living in them is not always easy. And, when one of us is not doing well, none of us are. This makes them a delicate, dynamic, messy, and endless work in progress.

This book centres around those moments when we must get involved, or call a child out on an unsafe, careless, or selfish action. Pitched well beyond the superficiality of making "happy families" or "obedient classes," this book dives into the colour and chaos of life. It provides guidance for navigating the commotion and the processes, as well as the grit required in the tougher moments. It's these moments that reveal what is really happening between children and their parents, educators, or carers. The book outlines a special set of attitudes and skills described as using our "soft eyes and warm hearts." In this space, we hold a child or teen accountable using an almost counterculture mindset. One that connects leadership and strength directly with kindness. This humane approach is more likely to leave young people in a position where they might want to feel responsible, make amends and changes, rather than being forced to. If we are to improve our relationships, outcomes, and futures with this generation of kids we must commit to truthful conversation, reflection, and preparation.

Written by trusted author Mark Le Messurier, an experienced teacher, counsellor, and public speaker, this is an essential guide for parents, carers, teachers, educational leaders, and allied health professionals responsible for the wellbeing of young people.

Mark Le Messurier is a teacher, counsellor, public speaker, and author. He works in private practice as a mentor to young people, a coach to parents, and a teacher educator. He is the recipient of the Australia Day Council's 2022 Senior South Australian of the Year award. His generosity and consideration for others was recognised as profound. He's helped many families, and has improved the self-worth, mental health, and life outcomes of children, adolescents, parents, and educators.

Guiding Kids Through the Tough Moments

Techniques to Build a Space Where Children Can Thrive

Mark Le Messurier

Routledge
Taylor & Francis Group
LONDON AND NEW YORK

Designed cover image: © Getty Images

First published 2023
by Routledge
4 Park Square, Milton Park, Abingdon, Oxon OX14 4RN

and by Routledge
605 Third Avenue, New York, NY 10158

Routledge is an imprint of the Taylor & Francis Group, an informa business

© 2023 Mark Le Messurier

British Library Cataloguing-in-Publication Data
A catalogue record for this book is available from the British Library

ISBN: 978-1-032-38649-2 (hbk)
ISBN: 978-1-032-38650-8 (pbk)
ISBN: 978-1-003-34671-5 (ebk)

DOI: 10.4324/9781003346715

Typeset in Optima
by SPi Technologies India Pvt Ltd (Straive)

Contents

Contents

Turns out, parenting and teaching are hard work, carry big responsibilities and have a huge intersect, notably how we treat children and adolescents in the tougher moments.

Some tools are taught to us by osmosis during our upbringing. And as you write, it is now a very different landscape for parents and teachers given what many experienced. Necessary new tools can be learnt, and that's what your book does and why it is so needed.

This book really nails it. It's current and based on your real, every-day work. I adore the case studies, anecdotes, and your conversational style. As I read it, I thought you were here with me. It was comforting!

I definitely think you should go ahead with it, Dad.

Kim Le Messurier, our daughter, harshest critic, scientist, married to Ayman and awesome mother to Tarik, Rami, and Lia. This was her response after reading the manuscript.

Author's note

I think of family as an intricate, evolving social and emotional world. This world exists to protect and nourish but the living in it is not always easy. And, when one of us is not doing well, none of us are. We are each different, and as we grow, we develop desires and attitudes to want different things at different times. Little wonder that in the space of a few hours we can shift from loving our children with the fullest of heart to wanting to give them away. These sets of feelings also apply to educators working with groups of children in classrooms and schools. All groups of young human beings are a dynamic, messy, and beautiful work in progress, with so many moving parts.

Intriguingly, this book centres around those moments when we must get involved, redirect, or call a child on an unsafe, careless, or selfish action. Many see such moments as tiresome, tedious, and repetitive. I adore them because what happens right here does not happen in a vacuum. These moments reveal our deeper mindset – whether we work in absolutes where there must be a winner and loser, what's really happening in the relationships, and how all of this converges when under pressure.

At the heart of this technique is a concept that connects leadership, composure, and strength directly with kindness. Holding a child or teen accountable in this way buoys their composure, keeps their dignity, and frees them from shame. It leaves them in a position where they might want to connect and make changes, rather than being forced to.

Once upon a time it was thought one should lead with strength, and kindness was a display of weakness. My experience is that this harmful attitude still lurks in the shadowy recesses of our minds today, especially when our children or students challenge us. If we are to shift patterns of behaviour, positively, from one generation of parents and educators to the next, it takes this kind of conversation, reflection, and preparation.

And now, you are gaining a sense of the precious space I want to build with you. This is so much more than a survival kit for growing healthy kids in the 21st century. The reality is that children today demand the "human stuff" from every adult involved in their life. And in a bid to connect, they will push buttons to witness the full range of human emotion so they can decide where to tap in, positively or negatively. Kids nowadays will not stand to be manipulated through cold, clinical, disconnected ways where adults flaunt the rules without relationship or respect. Their growing response to injustice and unkindness tells us this.

So, whether you are a parent, a foster parent, a carer, a teacher, an educational leader, a grandparent, or an allied health professional working with young people, walk with me to build authentic techniques where children can thrive.

About Mark Le Messurier

Mark Le Messurier is a teacher, counsellor, public speaker, and the author of 18 publications. He works in private practice as a mentor to young people, a coach to parents, and a teacher educator. He is often invited as a critical friend into schools who want to develop this deeper humane ethos. Mark regularly presents at conferences for universities, schools, for parent organisations, corporations, and interested groups throughout Australia and further afield.

He is the recipient of the prestigious Australia Day Council's 2022 Senior South Australian of the Year award. His generosity and consideration for others was recognised as profound, far reaching, and life changing. He's helped many families, and has improved the self-worth, mental health, and life outcomes of children, adolescents, parents, and educators.

One of Mark's speeches for the South Australian Australia Day Council is included because it sets the tone, perfectly, for this book.

> My passion is inspired by the hurt and confusion young people feel as they face unexpected, unfair, and unkind challenges in life. The books and programmes I've written illustrate my wild drive to share my understandings about young human beings with their significant others, namely their parents and educators. What follows is where our responsibility must sit, whether they're our children, or someone else's.
>
> Now it's our turn to be the adults. Whether we accept it or not we are holding the baton. And our children... well, they're just that... they are children, and they are relying on us. Their brains, bodies,

and spirit are in the process of precious construction. The atoms which merged to make them who they are did so like never before, and will never do so again. There will never be another of them anywhere in the universe. We want them to rejoice in their humanness, and know they are so much more than enough.

This is their birthright and our responsibility.

For reasons that you're all aware of – disadvantage, disability, disorder, trauma, and more – a large group of young people in our community struggle to connect, to learn and make meaningful friendships with peers. Yet, we know that continuing disconnection is a sure trigger for future mental health issues. Already we are losing too many young Australians each year because they struggle to connect, trust, share, or find services to help. To do too little, or nothing, against the menace of loneliness, sadness, depression, and suicide is unacceptable in a healthy, compassionate community.

Teaching young people the skills and the desire to live generously in a community is the essence of our "What's the Buzz?" programmes (www.whatsthebuzz.net.au). Huge shout out to my dear friend and writing partner Madhavi Nawana Parker. Our ambition was to create an evidenced-based social and emotional literacy programme that would bring kids, teens, and young adults together. It also needed to be accessible and affordable. So, we deliberately priced it at the very low end of the market.

And, 11 years on, "What's the Buzz?" is being used daily in more than 90 countries, in hundreds of schools world-wide, by hundreds of mental health and wellbeing practitioners, and in hundreds of community-based groups. Thousands of vulnerable young people have found, and continue to find, connection, friendship, purpose, and skill development through this simple, flexible programme that can be run by any adult whose heart and head is connected to the mental health of our youth.

I want to touch on the parents I work with. What a privilege it is to walk by their side. So many I see are in trouble because their kids have emotional and behavioural challenges. They do their best. But it's tough, lonely work, and they are sorely judged by others who don't understand. Experience teaches us that time, maturation, some targeted skill building, all wrapped in loving connectedness are the prime collaborators for healthy growth. I have shared many stories from parents in my new book, *Guiding Kids through the Tough Moments: Techniques to Build a Space Where Children Can Thrive*. I want their unrecognised courage, tenacity, and ingenuity to be understood and a source of strength to educators in schools, and to other parents.

Finally, what must I say about educators in schools? Many, not all, are miracle workers. The real miracle is that they reach incredible goals with young people and parents, just quietly, each day, without fanfare, without adequate training, without enough funding, and with too little support. They deftly guide young people towards realising goals, whether it is an adequate university entrance score, a high school certificate, a practical or technical pathway, or simply belief in themselves or in life after school.

But this success comes at a cost because the funding model for Australian schools is poor. As a community we have long accepted this, even though it is deeply morally wrong. Wouldn't you expect such highly complex places as schools, even smaller schools, to have a broad mix of social workers, youth workers, psychologists, counsellors, occupational therapists and speech pathologists on site for maintenance and intervention when needed? Instead, it falls to educators; a class teacher, a randomly available educator, a school support officer, a resourceful admin person, or to leadership to juggle yet another thing.

I admire educators who never lose sight of the powerful things they do. Like turning up to work each day. Painting a smile on their face and being ready, switching on their kindness and staying emotionally steady for everyone. And, some of the most powerful things they do appear insignificant and lost on those who do not understand. Yet, these educators know a powerful secret. It is that so many of their students thrive on their ordinary and generous habits because these habits provide emotional security and connection, and this is often a rarity in their lives.

I admire the educators who ride with young people, become their champions, and gift hope, and the possibility of recovery at future points in their life. Emotionally intelligent educators understand that now is not who a young person will be in the future, but what they do now sets their trajectory.

I am blessed to know you all, because every time our paths cross, you enrich and strengthen me.

Mark is on Facebook and can always be contacted by email – mark@marklemessurier.com.au or phone – +61459418909
www.marklemessurier.com.au
www.whatsthebuzz.net.au
www.teachingvaluesofbeinghuman.com.au

Intellectual property clause

Establishing intellectual property with absolute certainty is difficult. Many of the ideas within have arisen from generations of modifications and change. They are truly dynamic. It is common to see the wing of one idea transform into a new concept, depending on the need presenting at the time. This is the way it is when designing approaches to serve the diverse needs of young human beings. Wherever possible, the obvious and traceable sources have been acknowledged. If, by chance, an original source has been omitted, I sincerely apologise. The motivation has been to add to a repertoire of ideas, conversations, and activities that will benefit our children, or any young person trusted into our care.

Acknowledgements

Vanessa Bonaguro

Vanessa, I couldn't believe my luck when you said yes to being my first copy editor to my first manuscript. I knew that you'd embrace it and put your stamp on it with grammatical accuracy and empathetic wordsmithing. I'm deeply grateful that you also held me accountable over the book's tone, inclusivity, and engagement. Thank you for your kindness, wit, and wonderful eye for detail.

Deb Nurton

Once I finished my manuscript, I asked you to have a quick read and give me your instinctive reaction. You wrote, *"The book is amazing. It offers peaceful, gentle, thought-provoking support for parents. Good job!"* Thank you, Deb. I value your lived experience and that's why you are such a consummate therapist to children, coach to parents, and a "What's the Buzz?" facilitator in your own private practice – www.nurtureconnect.com.au.

Noni Le Messurier

Noni is our youngest daughter and colleague who runs her own practice. She is a skilled mentor to children and adolescents. In the early days I mentored her, and now she deftly encourages young people, families, and me. Noni has also done something quite remarkable. She has taken our global "What's the Buzz?" programme to new heights and runs older teen and young adult friendship/connect groups on a permanent, every week basis. Participants do not leave because they have found their tribe – www. nonilemessurier.com.au.

Sharon Palm

Sharon is my wife, finest friend, love of my life, and best critic. She runs our practice. That's a hard act. Sharon, thank you for the freedom you have given me to write over the years. I know that every word I have written took precious time away from us. Writing also means that my head is often preoccupied with how I might arrange thoughts and words and worry about how they'll be received. In the meantime, you found a brilliant mosaic artist living within. I love you and adore your work.

Lindy Petersen

I love you dearly, my friend. I have known you for many, many years and remain in admiration of you, and your work, as a clinical psychologist and author of *Stop, Think, Do*. The insights, compassion, and support you've given to families is inspirational. When I left the classroom to enter private practice you mentored me, coached me to run "Stop, Think, Do" groups with children, and generously referred clients. You had my back and still have it today. You are the reason I write! Thank you for your love and insights.

Lauren Eldridge Murray

You are so much more than a wonderful artist and a skilled layout designer. Your capacity to magically transform a manuscript into a visually rich book is breathtaking, and you do it seamlessly, intuitively, and gracefully every time. We have worked together through many projects including *Teaching Tough Kids, Teaching Values of Being Human*, the "What's the Buzz?" series, *Archies BIG BOOK of Friendship Adventures* and more. You shine in my heart as a resourceful confidant who always finds a way. Thanks for your great touches and tips on this one. You saved the day!

PREFACE: Where am I taking you?

A healthy perspective on childhood, and on how to raise and communicate with children, starts with a quick history lesson.

Once upon a time, for a long, long time, parents were encouraged to use sharp criticism, harsh words, hitting, and punishment, as the foundation to control children. This is mentioned in the English proverb "Children should be seen and not heard." It first appeared in *Mirk's Festial*, in 1450.

Before, and during, Victorian times, children would be beaten if they did even slightly mischievous things. The prevailing belief was a parent should be fearsome because this made them worthy of obedience. It was not in vogue for Victorian parents to display much affection towards their children. Consequently, they rarely kissed or hugged or spoke with their kids. Children had few toys, were dressed in restrictive clothing, and were expected to sit quietly without saying a word when adults were around. Poor Victorian children often came from big families packed into small, overcrowded, and neglected apartments. Their quality of living was not high. Consequently, it was usual to have children as young as six years working every day in factories and mines. The death toll for these children was extraordinary.

Around 1880 the law changed in the UK and children from the age of five years started to go to school. School, however, was based on a prison regime. Teachers were extremely strict, the day was long, and windows were high up, making it difficult for children to see out. The teaching was monotonous. Children sat in rows, in silence, and watched the teacher write on the blackboard. Then they would copy. School discipline was punishing. Children were regularly hit with a cane or strap for misdemeanours. Humiliation was imposed, sometimes by hanging children from the ceiling in a basket wearing a dunce cap. This was common and reflected the attitudes of society at the time.

Throughout the 1900s, the idea of childhood underwent an astounding transformation. Childhood began to be recognised as a separate space from adulthood. Jean Piaget's work, amongst others, showed that children progress through stages of cognitive development as they begin to comprehend the world (McLeod, 2020). Slowly, we learned that children were not born as little adults in small bodies. We began to appreciate what is appropriate for an adult is often not suitable for a child at all.

Then, just 30 years ago, world leaders made a historic commitment to children by adopting the United Nations "Convention on the Rights of the Child" (www.unicef.org.au/our-work/information-for-children/un-convention-on-the-rights-of-the-child). This ratified that all children require a separated, safe space and safe guardianship called childhood. A space where children were entitled to feel love, connection, and attachment from parents, from extended family, from teachers in schools, and from a community of caring adults because in this space, children thrive.

Yet, despite coming so far, I continue to witness too many adults, whether they be parents or educators, draw on this traditional combative style when the going gets tough. Would you like a little evidence?

What about when one of your children, or a student, decides not to listen, responds selfishly, defies your request, is rude, or worse? Remember this usually happens on top of an already overcommitted day, when you are juggling way too many balls, tired, and time is against you. So, what is your unconscious response in these hot and heavy moments? If honest, many of us click into a harsh way of thinking. Weirdly, this ornery mindset somehow appears tangled in our DNA from the past. But in that hot and heavy moment we instinctively grab for the punitive tools. We puff ourselves up, challenge them, invade their personal space, show anger, threaten to withdraw promises and privileges, or use every rule at our disposal, and for a short time may even withdraw our emotional connection because they made us cross or disappointed.

Ultimately, our children and students watch, and if exposed often enough, will learn to expertly use these very same power-based techniques themselves. Others will never use these techniques because they will tell you how it broke the precious bond between them and a parent, or a teacher. It is not human nature to feel loving, generous, or cooperative toward someone who uses scorn, punishment, and remoteness. A few of these children forever remain emotionally hurt. Consequently, they are more likely to suffer from anxiety, depression, trauma, and substance abuse troubles, and less likely to empathise with others or adopt normal patterns of moral behaviour.

Allow me to be crystal clear here. In a potentially risky, difficult, or dangerous moment, it is totally legitimate for an adult, parent, or educator, to urgently shout loudly, "Alexander, STOP!" to get Alexander's attention. Likewise, it is reasonable to eyeball a child or teen, use a convincing stare, a raised eyebrow, and snap at them to draw a line in the sand. You might curtly state, "Kim, that's not on." Or, "I won't ask again." Or, "Do what I'm asking because I'm about to flip my lid." What promotes this as leadership, rather than being overbearing, are two essential features. Firstly, the method is timely and genuinely justifiable in this circumstance. Your motivation is to lead a child through a precarious moment because they cannot do it independently. And what you have chosen and actioned is a calculated option from a repertoire of many options. Secondly, the basis of your approach is to maintain a precious bond between you and your child, or you and your students. There is no desire to punish, humiliate, hurt, or payback.

Cultivating techniques where children can thrive will feel uncomfortable for those who received harsh words, force, and punishment to be controlled in their formative years. My invitation is to coach you to change gears, and feel affection for your children or students when they are being stubborn, argumentative, even oppositional. This is what they need if we want to create trust and loyalty in our relationship. It is a call for us to be at our most respectful when, sometimes, they are at their least.

This technique stirs a train of thought, words, and actions that safeguard a young person's emerging spirit because we separate their behaviour from who they are, and who they might be in the future. We transport them into a precious space that gives them the freedom to think about what they have done and, perhaps, feel a little regret. On the other hand, when we push young people too far, too fast, they bunker down into self-protection mode. Their thoughts switch solely onto our heavy handedness, how unfair we were, and they lose sight of their involvement, their responsibility and what they could do to repair the situation.

My aim is to present 21st century humane techniques. Let us shake off past punitive practices as we now have accumulating evidence that these are no longer working in homes, and particularly in schools. These humane techniques will strengthen your communication and relationship with young people of all ages, especially those who have encountered difficult and traumatic histories. So, whether you are a parent, an educator in a classroom, or both, or more, my best advice is to:

Use the techniques sensibly. No technique is a substitute for warm, connected, and respectful exchanges.

While these are guiding principles that every parent and educator can rely on, this is truly a work in progress that takes time. There are no silver bullet solutions, although sometimes you will be beautifully surprised by positive emotional and behavioural shifts.

Make sure your approach is appropriate to the age and abilities of your child. Some children take longer to grow, to understand, to cooperate, and feel consideration towards others when it is most needed. This approach will eventually find success, but you may have to break your goals down, so each step is smaller, more consistent, and achievable.

Rely on your own common sense about how much you take on, and how much change your child can cope with. This trek has a different tempo for each child or student, and for each parent or teacher. Only you can gauge this.

Concentrate on the strategies that provide benefit and with which you feel comfortable.

With the above in mind, collect up the ideas you find enticing, gradually put them into practice, and enjoy the benefits your efforts will surely bring.

IN ADMIRATION: And from lessons learnt

The motivation for writing this book stems from the parents and educators who have allowed me into their lives over the years. I am forever grateful. I want to share your tenacity, courage, insight, and ingenuity so your best efforts become a source of guidance and strength to others. Thank you for taking me on the long ride with you. So many of you have shared enlightening ideas to skilfully manage the tricky emotions and behaviours of your children and students, despite it being "tough going" for you.

In respect to you as a reader, this is not a formulaic book about how to build "happy families" or "obedient students." I am not interested in the hollowness of "obedience." Such books do not reflect real life – what I have experienced in my own life or what I have seen in the lives of others. The truth is, we are all vulnerable learners with the capacity to improve – children, adolescents, and adults.

What I have witnessed from skilful parents and educators is the empathetic way they lead children and teens in the tough moments. They lead, even when under great pressure, by engaging their affection and deliberately reaching out. They may even place a reassuring arm on them. Their face softens, and they cleverly bring them emotionally closer. A parent might kiss them on the head or cheek and say, "That didn't go so well. We'll talk later. How can we fix things for now? I've got your back."

Later this parent, or teacher, will follow up. But in the meantime, by connecting in this way they have buoyed this young person's composure, helped them to keep their dignity, and freed them from the possibility of feeling shamed. They have cleverly left them in a position where they are more likely to feel a little remorse and want to take responsibility, rather than being pushed to.

In this space, the challenge for us is to dig a little deeper in the tougher or trickier moments, and use our strength, composure, and kindness. At the heart of these techniques are the humane principles – using "soft eyes and a warm heart." Principles where the ends never justify the means. Where there is a determination to be real, to connect, and persist.

A DECLARATION: My position on children and us

So, why do I have an image of a building "under construction" here?

Figure 0.1 Photo Building

This is a visible reminder that our children – their brains, bodies, and spirit – are in a precious process of construction. Their brains, quite invisibly, are undergoing a profound 30 year wire up.

Our children are genuinely naïve, experimenting and preparing for life. And as they learn and gather experience, they are bound to make poor judgments from time to time. It is what young inexperienced human beings do. You did it. I did it. We swung between being unbearable to virtuous in our search for identity, autonomy, and purpose.

Developmentally, at every age, there is a clumsy and vital tension between our children seeking greater autonomy and living within thoughtful limits we have created. Our mission is to support them to learn through every interaction, observation, success, and mistake, in a shame-free, fully supported environment.

Consequently, this is the perfect time to treat children with a deep reverence around consistency and persistence. How do we model and build these important foundations?

Consistency

We use language that is constructive, helpful, and connecting.

We give poised responses – a thoughtful beautiful blend of kindness, attachment, strength, and leadership.

We acknowledge the behaviours we value – carefully placed praise is the strongest shaper of desirable behaviours.

We notice their stressors and co-create opportunities for them to achieve greater success.

We teach new skills so they can function more effectively, everywhere.

Persistence

A while back, I had a consult with two parents about their sons. They had three boys aged 12, 13, and 15 years. The eldest boy frequently punched his brothers hard in the stomach to wind them. He thought it was funny because it got a big reaction as they doubled over and dropped to the floor. Mum did not think it was funny. Dad was unsure whether it was a problem. Mum was a school principal who worked enormous hours and Dad worked from home, part-time, as a consultant engineer. I cut to the chase and explained family was the place where each person's safety must be guaranteed, and this was dad's job.

"Well, how do you expect me to do that? I haven't got eyes in the back of my head!" he countered.

I agreed, and suggested he follow up every time there was a punching incident with a private conversation with the puncher as well as supporting the unsuspecting victim.

"Seriously? Every time? I've got better things to do than pander to this. It's just a phase!" He complained rolling his eyes, then shooting his wife a dark stare.

I boldly pushed on to where no other man had ever been with this father. "Yes, every time! And these private conversations must be private, must take no longer than three minutes, must start by you telling your son you love him, must reaffirm your family values and what you want, and you must stay gentle, connected, and good humoured!"

"How long for?" he asked.

"Ideally, forever. But if you're up for it let's give it a red-hot go for six weeks." I urged.

Unbelievably, he returned in six weeks. I opened the door to one of the best greetings I have ever received.

"I did it," he said, "I did exactly what you asked, over and over, and for the last fortnight we have been free of punching. You know, I grew up in a tough part of Glasgow. I can remember coming home to brag to dad about a fight I'd had as a kid and older. It was all around getting his approval. If he thought I'd done well there'd be a smirk of approval on his face. If I hadn't won, then he'd send me back again to square up. I think it got into my DNA and messed up my thinking. It was pretty dysfunctional."

This amazing man's love for his boys carried his heart and soul into this experiment. He persisted for the boys, for his wife and for his family. I know that his resolve saved much more than he will ever know.

Remember, every day is a new day, and with it comes the opportunity to restart a promise you've made to yourself even though it may have fallen short the day, or days, before. New days invite our hopes and wishes to become real. Please persist!

FAMILY
An evolution and revolution

This chapter is written with great respect to parents and teachers because anything that parents face with their children, teachers face in schools with students and families. Parenting and teaching have become infinitely more intricate and fluid in such a short space of time. An ever-increasing flow of information, misinformation, and influence arrives at a frenetic pace over various platforms, whether we want it or not. Such cerebral overload fires up anxieties, obsessions, fantasies, opinions, and behaviours. Yes, it feels like we blinked, and the world changed. While there are so many more choices, it must be said, that these options also bring complexities that impact heavily on children, parents, educators, homes, and schools. What parents and teachers navigate today is a new, supercharged "normal"; a normal hardly recognised by previous generations. The overriding theme here is – "Our children need us on their side." Today parents and teachers require such a sophisticated set of interpersonal skills to communicate with young people in their care. To be connected, kind, and emotionally reliable is a must, but to be able to calmly switch and lead decisively, with strength and compassion, in opportune moments, is equally necessary.

A once upon a time family

Not that long ago, a family was more easily defined. There was a stereotyped model called the "nuclear family" that the vast majority identified with. This was an idealised family group consisting of a man and a woman and their

DOI: 10.4324/9781003346715-1

two children, preferably a boy and a girl. And each adult in the partnership took on parenting roles that were set in stone. Back then a father's role was to provide for his family and have brief interactions with them. He went to work early, came home late, and the measure of his success was his job and the family's income. A mother's role was just as distinct. Parenting was referred to as women's work. Marriages often stayed together even though couples, and their children, may have been desperately unhappy.

As a result, generations of children grew up hungering for the attachment of a father they barely knew. Generations of fathers were oblivious to the benefits of being emotionally connected to their children. A few recognised it and did what they could. Seventy-five-year-old Jim eloquently reflects such thoughts with his young granddaughter in the TV series, *Breeders*:

> I've never told your dad I love him. Mad isn't it really? I've never kissed him. I've returned a hug, but I've never offered one. It's because of my age, and I suppose my background. All men were buttoned up like that in the old days. Me and your dad were the same for years, decades. And now suddenly you have to be open and emotionally intelligent...
>
> (*Breeders*, 2020: season 1, episode 9)

Please do not make the mistake that this attitude is strictly confined to an older generation. It is not. Here is a case study about Matt, who is a client. Matt is 34 years old, a great person and married to Jo. They have a six-year-old son and an eight-year-old daughter.

Walking in the footprints of my father

When Matt's daughter, Annie, is upset it does not matter what he is doing. He will stop, pick her up, cuddle her, and pop her onto his lap. Matt will ask, *"Tell me what's wrong, Annie? How are you feeling? What's made you feel like this?"* He'll say, *"Don't worry, Daddy's got your back, and we can fix it."* And he'll take all the time in the world to help her recover.

On the other hand, when little Zac comes to him crying, Matt behaves differently. Zac is just six. Matt admits he has got an inbuilt timer of about 36 seconds worth of patience for Zac's upset feelings because he is a boy, and he needs to learn to get on with it.

Straight away Matt will say to Zac:

"What's wrong?"
"Why are you crying?
"Hold your head up. Look at me."
"I said, what's wrong. Tell me what's wrong?"
"I can't understand what you're saying while you're blubbering."
"Stop crying!"
"Come on, pull yourself together and talk to me like a man."

Matt is aware of this; he is on to it and is changing it. He thinks he was walking in the footprints of his dad because when Matt was a boy, he was not allowed to cry or to express his feelings. He was taught to suck it up, swallow and supress those feelings. Act like a man.

We now understand the real value of males being optimistically and emotionally involved in the lives of their children. When done well, a deeper involvement by a father takes nothing away from a mothers' unique contribution to her children and family, it simply adds richness. It turns out that a connection between a father and a child during pregnancy, even though the father cannot touch, hear, or see the child, has a lifelong positive effect on the father, mother, and child.

Not that long ago, a new focus and language about how children should grow socially, emotionally, intellectually, even spiritually emerged (Goleman, 1996). We started to learn that to give young human beings the best potential to thrive we must pack their early years with plenty of opportunities to be loved, led, empowered, and stimulated. However, understanding this and paying attention to a child's internal world was not an easy ask for parents who never received this, or missed out on strong emotional bonds with their parents. The pressure to be a different or a better parent started to grow. Parents were no longer satisfied with the status quo. Our latest generations of parents have been subjected to many, many valuable ideas and so much chatter about it abounds, but real change in attitudes is not easy.

Today, there are no limits to describe the nature, spirit, and beauty of family. It comes in varying shapes, sizes, and capacities, together with an array of beliefs, ethnicities, and spiritual values.

"Family" isn't defined only by last names or blood; it's defined by commitment and by love. It means showing up when they need it most. It means having each other's backs. It means choosing to love each other even on those days when you struggle to like each other. It means never giving up on each other!

(Dave Wills, an American voice actor, writer, and producer)

We freely use the terms "blended family," "LGBTQIA+ family," "co-parenting," "single parent family," "extended family," "family of choice," "faith family," and more. Family members may be related by blood, marriage, or adoption – contractually and lawfully bound together, but equally, they do not need such formal bonds to create the building blocks of a family. More than anything, family provides a sacred space for this unique event we call childhood. In this space, children should be guaranteed the chance to find their identity, be heard, be curious, feel accepted, and supported as they investigate their emerging world. This "rite of passage" demands parents lead, and sometimes walk shoulder to shoulder with their children on this amazing journey to adulthood.

This freer, more progressive, less rule-bound spirit of family and community does not come without complications, pressures, and consequences for both children and parents.

Separations, divorce, and relocation

Today, many children and young people must deal with moving between homes and parents due to separations and divorce (Halford, 2018; Australian Bureau of Statistics, 2019). Children become conflicted, confused, and traumatised. But it is not the separation or divorce which does this to them. It is the continuing bickering, antagonism, even hatred, between parents that eats away at them. The separation of parents, the loss of one's home and bedroom, let alone the loss of a beloved pet and the dream of a perfect family, are significant losses for a child, and for parents too. Suddenly two combined incomes are lost as well, and with this comes single parent financial hardship and single parent poverty. Bitter experience has taught us that too many children know too much about their parents' personal relations and financial difficulties. This sets them up to take sides, worry and be part of a conflict they do not need to be a part of. Some children face a fiery baptism into a blended family where they share spaces and belongings that are too small and too few. The lucky few find a comfortable niche and feel loved. The truth is, divorce takes more love and care than marriage because children's future emotional health depends heavily on how it is handled by parents.

Abuse, trauma, and child protection

Australian research indicates that 40% of children experience at least one form of childhood abuse (Smith, 2021). Is this figure greater than it was 20 years ago? No one really knows for sure, because there has always been an ominous silence and shame around disclosing. What we do know is that when young people are exposed to traumatic situations their emotions and behaviour become far more complicated, and fast. Trauma is the result of a single stressful event, or a series of them. It is a "failure to recover," and this allows the trauma to be re-enacted, over and over, often with lifelong consequences. The result is that some children become less capable of coping with adversity as they grow up. Young people who have experienced trauma and loss in their short lives often have developmental vulnerabilities and challenges in three key areas: executive functioning, emotional self-regulation, and psychological development (for greater detail see https://developingchild.harvard.edu/science/key-concepts/executive-function/).

Those of us who have worked with children and families for some time believe there are more children with complex needs at younger ages than ever. Today, one third of South Australian children are the subject of a notification to the Department for Child Protection by the age of ten years. One third of these notifications met the threshold for further assessment and response (The South Australian Commissioner for Children and Young People, 2021).

Self-harm

Today, the act of self-harming is widespread in children and adolescents. Self-harming takes the form of rubbing, grinding, cutting, or burning one's skin or taking non-lethal overdoses. Perhaps 10% to 20% of young people self-harm. This means about two students in every classroom have self-harmed or will self-harm. It is hard to know exact figures because many deliberately do not seek support due to secrecy, humiliation, and embarrassment. Most health experts say it is on the rise (Australian Institute of Health and Welfare, 2020). Most young people say they started to hurt themselves around the age of ten years because it provided a temporary relief from the emotional pain they were feeling and was something practical they could do.

Self-harming is widely discussed on social media platforms. On the one hand, healthy support and care can be offered by online communities. Then, on the other hand, there is a view that some post to improve their social status. This then creates a worrying ripple effect on others. Some children feel overwhelmed by those who engage in this behaviour, some feel a compulsion to emulate and compete, and others express outright anger that their friends do such an unthinkable act. It leaves parents feeling terrified and powerless. While self-harm is not a suicide attempt, it must be taken very seriously and requires an emotionally intelligent response from a parent and a mental health professional. We are learning that young people who self-harm have an elevated risk of suicide, later, compared with those who do not self-harm.

A despairing view of the world

We want our kids to develop an optimistic outlook on life because optimism fuels resilience. After all, resilient people make better choices, experience better physical and mental health, live longer, and are more satisfied with their relationships and life.

But in my individual sessions with young people I am seeing a troubling trend. Increasingly, they steer the conversation towards a despairing view of the world. They grieve over the grim future triggered by climate change and the lack of international unity to slow global carbon emissions. Issues such as deforestation, the loss of biodiversity, and the fear of nuclear attacks, especially since Russia invaded the Ukraine and threatened nuclear retaliations, are in the forefront of their minds. The COVID-19 pandemic has not done them any favours either. And it is not the pandemic that amplifies their anxiety, it is the confusing array of enraged opinions. Concerns also include the personal cost of maintaining an online presence, online threats and harassment, income inequality and housing affordability, food, water, and power security, and feeling small in a big world.

This creates worry, anxiety, despondency, and depression in some. In others, it exaggerates an appetite to do things that distract, and instantly gratify, because there may not be a tomorrow anyway. Endeavours range from dishing out hate, secretly from the privacy of one's bedroom, to openly posting TikTok videos that humiliate, discredit, and hurt.

The truth is the 24/7 media cycle never stops. It continuously feeds into our naturally negative bias with the power to grow a sense of helplessness. I have a couple of tips that I often share. Coach kids to dwell on the joys and pleasures in their life. Encourage them to let the happy and satisfying feelings sink in. Support them to find ways to connect with community. To put their energy towards participation whether it is with family, extended family or volunteering in an association or community organisation that makes a difference. Help them to find a cause at a local level, where political, environmental, or social changes can be made.

Competitive and exclusive parenting

Over the past five years, I have hosted a parent discussion group at a local community centre. Throughout the year, 15 of us would meet each month, discuss a parenting topic, share our thoughts and feelings, build friendship, find solace, and consider possible solutions. I have adored the bonds we forged with each other. May I share the two persistent themes that crop up?

The first was the competitive pressure parents place on each other. One mother of two young children initiated a passionate discussion seized on by all. She announced she had turned off notifications from her "Mum Facebook group" because posts teetered between being supportive and highly competitive, and it provoked her anxiety! The discussion group agreed and raised the trends of signing up babies to exclusive childcare, swim centres, and private schools, years into the future. As well, there was the competition about whose child got their teeth first, when they sat up, when they started on solid food, and started walking and talking, let alone the sleep contest. Sadly, all of this of this is done as if there is a leader board, and there is a mad scramble to get to the top to prove parental worthiness. The consensus was that any parent who touts their child being ahead of the developmental curve is expressing their own anxieties. The talk then turned to being kinder to themselves and to each another. Do we need reminding that human beings are wonderfully diverse and grow differently?

The second theme concerns exclusive parenting, or a style of parenting where others are judged on differences and excluded. I refer to many of the young people I mentor, very affectionately, as "tough kids." I do not mean they present themselves as tough, hardened kids at all. What I do mean is they do life much tougher than their counterparts. Their lives are consumed by the unpredictability of their functioning: they struggle to delay gratification, listen, and filter out distractions, process new information, remember, plan, persist, adapt to change, keep track of time, and self-regulate emotion and behaviour. They also make life so much tougher for those who care for them and educate them. Many of these beautifully diverse children and teens join our "What's the Buzz?" social skills and friendship groups. The kids work with us each week, and while they do, their parents use this time to connect, debrief, laugh, exchange stories and ideas, and find strength in each other. These parents do their best. But it's tough, lonely work, and they are often sorely judged by other parents who don't understand. It is remarkable to watch their friendships grow, and 15 years later we have groups of mothers who have remained together and catch up for a girl's weekend away several times each year. They meet because they understand each other, find solace in one another, and know the deep value of inclusion.

"Monkey see, monkey do" parenting

"Monkey see, monkey do" was a further theme raised in our parenting group. This is an idiom that refers to the act of imitating something (in this case how our parents raised us) without understanding why they did it, why it worked, whether it worked, and what the consequences might be. Do you believe you parent in much the same way as you were parented? Or are you now using a warmer and more connected approach? And what's your default position when under pressure? Is it to snap back to exactly what you experienced? Parenting perceptively with "soft eyes and a warm heart" does not just happen. The group believed it is possible to escape the way we were parented, but the stamp on us from our childhood experience is enduring. Without a little courage to try things differently, some honest reflection, a smattering of parent education and support from wise friends, we either embrace what we received or flip right over and completely oppose it.

Choice or no choice?

A perfect example of flipping against the parenting style experienced in their formative years was illustrated by a father of two young girls. I was in full flight in the middle of a parenting workshop when he playfully called out, *"Hey, Mark? Dunno where it came from, but I must have received an email that said I have to justify every small decision, every choice, and every request I give to my girls. This is what I do. Truth is, that it's doing my head in and now I've created an expectation. I think I have utterly overreacted to what happened to me as a child. My brother and I were subjected to nothing but a heavy-handed parenting style, and we never had choices."*

The point here is that a lot of us don't see we have a choice. Instinctively we either follow, or flip, the parenting style we experienced in our early years. None of us want our kids to face the unfairness, heavy handedness, or the humiliations we endured, so we become driven to generate a contrasting style as a replacement. Yet this opposing style, while different, can be just as problematic. It is reactionary, rather than values-based and considered.

An over-scheduled generation of children

I regularly work with parents who organise one, even two, planned activities for their children every day of the week. Their children are strapped into a white knuckled weekly rollercoaster ride that is fast and furious, and relentless on both child and adult.

There are two observations I must share, and with great respect and no blame.

Firstly, there are parents who have been fortunate to receive funding for therapies through the National Disability Insurance Scheme (NDIS) because their children have been identified with disabilities and neurodivergence early on. Early intervention is always best, but there is a temptation for parents to sign up to as many therapies as possible while the funding exists. I see many relationships under serious strain as loving parents try to keep up with therapies. I also understand that early on is a time when parents are at their most vulnerable, and with therapies being pushed so hard, this can cause an over-focus on what's missing in their child and how to "repair," "fix-up," or "top them up."

This is the moment to consider the term neurodivergence. It attempts to describe neurotypes that diverge from the supposed norm. For example, ADHD, Autism, PTSD, dyslexia, dyspraxia, dyscalculia, mental health conditions, intellectual disability and more. Gradually, we are understandinging that such differences in individual emotional and behavioural traits are the result of physical differences in brain structures. A neurodivergent brain is built and wired-up differently, so it processes and interacts with the world differently. It will always do so because its operating system is a beautiful variation that beats uniquely to a different human rhythm.

The fact is that our neurodivergent young people are not broken and do not need to be fixed. I agree, early intervention is best, but we must not lose the deep meaning of 'neurodivergence'. To highlight this, no one ever grows out of autism. Children with autism grow up to be adults with autism. So, let's value this and help them grow into it.

I recently heard a well-meaning, albeit frustrated, principal say to an 11-year-old, "You need to all of the maths problems because in real life, there won't be any short cuts." The truth is this kind of analogy and hurdle jumping isn't helpful or accurate. Yes, we want this child to develop maths skills, but there is a planned, progressive, and humane way to do this. By the way – 'there are always short cuts in real life too!'

Over time, most of us shift our thinking from this incapacitating 'deficit model', heaping the immediate pressure of conformity onto kids, to a much healthier strength-based model. Experience teaches us that time, growth, maturation, some targeted skill building, all wrapped in loving connectedness are the primary collaborators to leading a life with meaning and purpose. Let's build school and family environments that actively teach kids that they are enough, we value them for who they are and there is real hope about their future. Let's also embrace their beautifully diverse abilities, enjoy their quirkiness, and rejoice in their individuality.

"How sick am I?"

CASE STUDY

It was the first time I'd met Max. He was ten years old. I'd met his mother at a previous appointment where she explained Max's history, challenges, interests, and strengths. Max happily bounced into my room. As we sat down,

I smiled, and he flashed an accepting grin straight back. I asked if he'd mind holding on for just a moment while I finished writing a note. He said that he didn't mind and looked around the room.

While I was writing Max quietly asked, "How sick am I?"

"You're not sick at all, Max, what makes you ask that?"

"I must be, because mum takes me to lots of therapies so someone can make me better."

Max's comment reminds us that when children are carted, too often and indiscriminately, from one therapist to another for too long they can develop an "in therapy" attitude about themselves. This approach delivers a message that something is wrong with them. It reinforces that someone else, or some new slick programme, will take responsibility for their challenges and will miraculously fix their life. A better approach is where the focus is firmly on the child's existing strengths and positive qualities. We use these attributes as a foundation to improve their quality of life and reduce challenges.

Second are the parents who believe in keeping their kids relentlessly busy and developing underlying skills and talents to semi-professional levels. I adore the idea of children becoming the best they can be, but reject the unbearable intensity inspired by a chase for making every moment "happy" or "productive" for a child. A few of the young people I see are caught up in this, and yearn to get off the rollercoaster and have an afternoon or two free, just to mooch. A variation of this are the children who see a parent (traditionally it has been their fathers, but this is changing) one weekend every fortnight. Mostly, they look forward to it and so does this parent. The parent may feel as though their children's experiences over the weekend must be perfect, idyllic, and memorable. And for this to occur, this parent works tenaciously to over-deliver non-stop activities, fabulous fun, no boundaries, and no conflict.

The consequence of keeping up with this, or keeping up with a hectic lifestyle, is that children rarely hear "no" from them. While all of this comes from a place of great love, these parents are indulging their kids with a permissive style because it "keeps the peace" or makes life on the never-ending rollercoaster slightly easier or more bearable. The result is these children experience too few boundaries, or rubbery and negotiable boundaries, which builds a sense of entitlement and false expectation. They expect what they want and will fight hard for it citing their rights when they hear "no" from parents, their other parent, and teachers.

Sadly, unintentionally, they are robbed of precious experiences that teach them the skills of appreciation, humility, gratitude, and acquiescence. When such attitudes and skills are not practiced and reinforced, over and over, in the early years, they remain noticeably underdeveloped and it is the children who will face the deceptive and devastating aftereffects of this.

Screens and cognitive overload

What about the unparalleled surge of online choices in the last decade or so? When it comes to devices and screens, there have never been so many tempting choices, and this comes at a time in our children's lives when their "self-regulatory on/off switches" are a long way from being, neurologically, wired up. And that is why switching off screens is the basis for a perfect storm in so very many homes.

The pull to screens has long been precisely engineered so it is both captivating and inescapable. And the attraction is not simply confined to children and adolescents. Too many adults are now deeply caught up with gaming, social media, and employment responsibilities on their devices. The cost of this is that valuable little parcels of time that once used to be spent with our children, partners, and family are insidiously swallowed up. A parent's thoughts and time are now shared between what is happening on their device and being connected to the people who matter most in their lives. The lure of the cyber world, work and play, applies a relentless pressure on real-world participation and engagement.

Suddenly, in that moment, when the kids or our partner make a request, we feel interrupted and put upon. This is because we are forced to tear our attention away from what is happening on our device, to a situation we must abruptly switch on to. In this moment, our loved ones receive only part of our listening and part of our attention. Our vague or irritated tone of voice hints at our detachment. We are short-changing them, and ourselves. We each know this is real but dismiss it by convincing ourselves we can multitask.

An email from 15-year-old Eloise

"Dear Mark,

Like everyone else my age I spend a lot of time on lots of social media platforms. This is a big part of my generation's life. This is what we do. It is proof of our existence and I hate it. It's doing my head in. But it's an inheritance we're tied to. I watch my friend's posts and they make me feel small, empty, and nothing. Here are my usual string of thoughts as I read their posts:

Their life's perfect
Mine's not
Mine's nothing. I'm nothing
Why do I do this?
I can't do this anymore
There's no point
I shouldn't even try
I like no one
No one likes me
I want out
There's no feeling in this
I should cut myself to feel
I hate this all this. It's too much
I have no purpose
I'm a waste of space

Mark? I'm now starting to feel scared. How do I stop these thoughts? How do I separate real life from social media, or is social media real life for my generation?"

We are the first generation to parent children growing up with this technology, deliberately built to be irresistible. Never before have parents and kids been swamped by an extraordinary level of cognitive input and choices through such an enticing and easily accessible medium. As Eloise points out, there are frightening costs attached.

As loving parents, I urge you to keep your eye on the greatest prize. This is to maintain a buoyant, connected relationship with your kids, so you can chip away at helping them navigate a balance between screens and real-life friendships and obligations. And, to do this our kids need us firmly on their side – not against them, fighting them, being superior, and belittling their interest, the true value of which we may not entirely grasp. When we blatantly fight them, we turn their desire for screens into a crazed chase for forbidden fruit. As soon as they know you "hate screens" and you are "the screen police," the battle is on. Yes, limits are necessary, but the goals and method must be all about "managing time" and how to "nurture great mental health."

Sexual and gender identity

Parents have long had conversations with their children around sex education and health. Today such conversations must also include sexual and gender identity. Discovering their own sexuality includes understanding who and how they are attracted to another and there are many ways to express and label this compared to past times.

Very quickly parents are compelled to realise there is much more to gender identity than being male or female. The transgender umbrella includes those who don't identify with the gender they are assigned at birth, and includes many identities.

Compassionate parents do not want their child to bury their sexual or gender identity as this wreaks havoc on self-esteem, mental and physical health. Parents are learning that we do not know why some people are "straight" and others fall under the LGBTQIA+ umbrella, but our sexuality is not a choice. Parents are also discovering the appropriate pronouns and language associated with the LGBTQIA+ communities as it helps our kids to see us as inclusive and respectful.

The truth is, children, teens, and young adults are discovering that they don't always feel comfortable in their own skin and part of this is looking at how they identify with the world and themselves. Everyone has the right to feel comfortable and to be accepted for who they are.

A sign of the times

One of the most exclusive and conservative boys-only colleges in my city has openly accepted a Year 12 student who now wishes to be identified as a female. Alice is the first student to transition whilst at the college and she began at the school in the early years. It is her desire to remain because of the unwavering support she has received from friends, peers, and staff. She delivered a powerful speech to 150 classmates to explain that she is transgender, now identifies as a woman, and wishes to be known as Alice. She said, "This is who I am… this is who I have always been. So, it's not a transition as it might appear to be but very much a statement of who I am." The response from the Year 12 cohort was touching, respectful, and highly supportive.

Alice continues to be counselled by skilled professionals, both within and outside the college. The school is currently working with Alice to resolve issues relating to uniform and presentation, so that she can express her transition in her way. The headmaster said that while there was overwhelming support, he expected some resistance, but had a clear sense of what is right and felt diversity and inclusiveness are far more than words in a policy.

How uplifting to see such connected levels of support for Alice. This story makes my heart sing! Only a few years ago, coming out at school was frowned upon because reactions were usually negative and hurtful.

The most important thing we are learning is to accept a young person's sexual or gender identity. A young person's identity should never break or diminish our relationship with them, whether we are their parent, educator, or part of their extended family. Almost invisibly, our acceptance begins well before they question or declare it. It begins early on when they watch and listen to us respond to any kinds of injustice. When a young person asks questions about the sexual or gender identity of others, keep in mind that they may be questioning themselves. The quality of our response is likely to determine if we will be the person they will talk to when they are ready. To finish up, one of my mid-teen-aged clients is transitioning. His father had not said much about it but had been quietly supportive. He was a chocolatier, and everything fell beautifully into place for Mickey when Dad came home with chocolates he had made in LGBTQIA+ colours as a gift for him.

An anxiety epidemic?

The resilience of young people, or their capacity to cope, is now under serious threat in Australia. Among young people aged 14–17 years, one in five have emotional, mental health, and/or behavioural challenges (Swan, 2020).

In this same age group, suicide and self-inflicted injuries are causing the largest burden on the health system, followed by anxiety and depressive disorders. More and more children are displaying anxiety and depression. Currently 7% of Australian children aged 6–11 meet the criteria for diagnosable anxiety in Australia, and thousands more suffer from anxiety, as a direct response to what is happening in their lives (Hermant, 2017).

The world does seem less safe than it once was. Parents have every reason to feel "risk averse." What parents are hearing now is, "If you're not anxious, you're not paying attention to your kids!" I adore this saying because it urges us to be in tune with our children, but for others the interpretation is to over-protect their children. And, when over-protection gets in the way we systematically steal precious opportunities from our children to face difficult situations and learn they can handle them. Once we place young people on the slippery slope of over-protection, we see them become highly reliant on an adult to fix problems they could fix. This does not give a child the opportunity to face difficult situations and learn they can handle them. Their perseverance and resilience disappear and are replaced by fearful and dependent thinking. Odd, unexpected, and stressful events will surely come our way. And, as strange as it sounds, the development of resilience does require challenge, change, and some emotional distress. After all, if we never faced disputes, conflict, and hardship, we would never learn how to work with them, cope with them, and recover from them.

"A mother and daughter's conversation."

I adored this exchange during a consult, and with permission, have almost remembered it word perfect! It concerns the emotional anguish a mother's 15-year-old son was managing. What a privilege to be part of such a beautiful conversation; it reminded me that our pain is ours, their pain is theirs, and that is the irresistible natural order!

Grandmother:	"I don't know what to do right now, either. The answers will come, they always do. It will take time for him to reach the other side of the upset he's going through."
Mother:	"But I'm his mum. I should be able to help him. That's my job."

Grandmother:	"Oh, if only it were that easy. If only we could wipe away every tear our children cry or kiss their hardship away. If only we could keep them from falling. But they must fall, get hurt, get bruised, feel pain, then learn to cope, and only then can grow."
Mother:	"I just want him to talk to me about it."
Grandmother:	"Be patient. All you can do is be there, right beside him, for when he reaches out. Your job is to love him and resist the impulse to fix it for him. This is his learning."

Learning to accept that space where we feel "uncomfortable" or at a "loose end" is a gift to be cultivated. It does, however, take patience, a little courage, and persistence to live it well. In essence, this is the art of being resilient; acknowledging one's emotions, knowing support is available when you want it, and staying in the uncomfortable space for a while, because it helps to reflect on what happened, and what is best to do next.

The impact of COVID-19 on families

At the time of writing, we are over two years into the pandemic. All of us have experienced the new world of border closures, lockdowns, restrictions, QR codes, social distancing, masks, working remotely, school closures and online schooling from home, PCR and rapid antigen testing, and living in isolation or "iso." And every one of these COVID-19-related experiences stirs uncertainty, fear, and anguish. For some of us the impact has been severe; we have lost jobs, lost incomes, lost homes, lost freedoms and choices, lost physical contact with extended family and friends, lost treasured family members and lost the futures we were anticipating. With this said, when our Australian experience is compared to what has occurred globally, we are grateful and reminded of the benefits living in Australia brings.

One thing is for sure; not knowing when this pandemic will end, what twists and turns await us, and when normality will return is hugely anxiety and depression provoking. We now have evidence of skyrocketing mental health issues triggered by COVID-19, and frankly, we should not be surprised (Hand et al., 2020). What is more anxiety provoking than the thought of being let go from work, losing one's income, not being able to meet financial commitments, and losing choices, identity, and lifestyle? Whether this emerges as a reality is not the only point. A significant point is that the fear of the unknown looms over many as a heavy, constrictive gloom that eats away at the joy life should bring.

Yet, there are some valuable lessons we have learnt from the hardships instigated by the pandemic. Firstly, that positive experiences can be made, and can emerge, within what seems like a negative and threatening space. My friend, Madhavi Nawana Parker, wrote this reassuring rally to parents about "Online home schooling" during this tough period. She urges parents to be kinder to themselves, seize on the joyful moments that naturally arise, and make them count! Savour Madhavi's wisdom because it is well beyond "Online home schooling." It is universal advice about modelling a good life (not a perfect one) with our children, so they learn how to do the same.

Online home schooling

It's okay if you've had enough of online home schooling.

You have permission to be human.
To not be perfectly tolerant and wise, every second.
You have permission to feel frustrated.
To be counting down the days.

It's hard on you and your children.
So, it's time to cut yourself some slack.
If you're finding it hard, you're not alone.
Grab moments as they bob up to reconnect with yourself and your children.

Few people can cope with being online all day in front of a screen, day after day with a smile on their face.
So, slow down and take a rest when you can.
And you know what matters way more than completing yet another activity sheet?
Your children's connection with you.
Knowing you love and like them even when they're not performing to your expectations.

While it's hard on us, it's hard on them too.
They miss their friends.

They miss their teachers (who are trained to teach, unlike us).
They miss being your child and not your student.
So, hang in there, beautiful people.
Grab joy where you can.
Surrender to the fact you're not going to get to the end of your
    "to-do list" until they're back at school.

Accept what's happening.
Try not to resist it.
Resisting reality doesn't make sense … and it will exhaust you.
Instead, tell yourself, "this is not an emergency."

Breathe.
Pause.
Play music in the background.
Change the scenery (we did maths in a cafe, grammar in the garden
    and now we're in the library doing punctuation).

Am I exhausted? Yes.
Am I completely behind at work? Yes.
Do I love my children more than life itself? Yes.
So, I'm going to keep breathing and keep smiling at how hilarious
    all this is.
Because I've taken on the responsibility of teacher and I have no
    qualifications to teach.
Instead, I practice keeping my cool, and when I mess up, I'll apologise
    and ask, "how I can make it better?"

Children are divine, forgiving creatures.
Take care beautiful people. You can do this.
    Madhavi Nawana Parker (www.positivemindsaustralia.com.au)

Secondly, being locked down, having to isolate and enduring social restrictions highlighted what Professor Julianne Holt-Lunstad and the World
Health Organisation had been telling us prior to COVID-19 (Holt-Lunstad
et al., 2017). They predicted our newest global health threat. It is depression
inspired by loneliness.

What we have learnt first-hand is that each of us need deep connection
to family, friends, and significant others because this is THE protective factor

against loneliness. Loneliness drastically increases risks for sadness and depression, cardiovascular health, premature death, and a faster rate of cognitive decline and dementia. Feeling disconnected, according to Holt-Lunstad, is equivalent to the dangers of smoking 15 cigarettes a day, twice as toxic as obesity, as lethal as alcoholism, and the negative effects are greater than those of air pollution or leading a totally sedentary life (Kurzgesagt, 2019). Most vulnerable are children, teens, and the elderly. But we discovered none of us were immune.

On this, I was left in awe how some of the families I know quickly adapted to our "new normal," displaying remarkable creativity and deep emotional intelligence. More than a few took to growing herbs, flowers, and veggies, raising chickens, albeit in tiny back, side, and front yards. This set the scene for them to garden, harvest food, cook, discuss, learn, and eat meals together. Many of my families shared meals with friends and extended families online, and ate, chatted, and drank together. As well, they deliberately set up opportunities to walk together, play board, card, and video games, and watch movies while ensuring everyone had their own space and privacy at times. Some brought pets, especially dogs, into their lives, often for the first time. One of my clients, a 15-year-old, felt his family had been blessed by the chance to have a dog. According to him, everyone had developed their own bond with Rosie, and she had somehow improved the quality of the family's relationships and communication. He said, "Home feels warmer and softer because of Rosie."

Many families also discovered that structures and routines really do help children to feel safer, happier, and more cooperative. And within our "new normal" they also learnt to take care of themselves so they could maintain strength to care for those they love. The pandemic is unwanted but has offered a unique moment in time to re-think our role and responsibility to build "mental health hygiene principles." These are the everyday thoughts, actions, and activities we do to encourage our own, and our children's, psychological and emotional health.

Mental health hygiene principles

ACTIVITY

Can we guarantee against mental health difficulties in our children? No, we cannot. Some mental health issues arise from the unexpected twists and turns of life, and associated traumas. Others are outside of our control and are heavily influenced by illness, disability, deficits, disorders, loss, conditions, and so much more. However, by incorporating these mental health hygiene principles into our lives these behaviours can be learnt and become habitualised by our children. And if by chance your child experiences a spell of mental health difficulty, this framework can offer protective patterns to aid their recovery.

Isn't it ironic that much of our children's mental health hinges on our awareness, understanding, and modelling of these basic and healthy principles? So, in no particular order, here is my brief 12-point checklist of mental health hygiene principles. Keep your own checklist in mind and compare! Then be sure to model and coach them to your children.

Point 1 – "A problem shared is a problem halved"

When the going gets tough coach your kids to share their thoughts with family and friends. Family and friends are such a blessing because they love us and want to participate in our lives. They remind us not to take ourselves too seriously, to recognise the perfectionist within, not to over-think, and always provide us with a sprinkle of optimism and a sparkle of hope.

Point 2 – Get rid of household drama

Do away with the unnecessary drama that plays out too often in too many families. Instead, model how we slow down, breathe, and self-regulate our emotions. Do away with overreacting and becoming too picky, too shouty, too controlling, too dominating, too angry, and too frightening because when we do this, we increase the stress hormones circulating in our children's brains. Consequently, with the constant release of cortisol, brain growth runs the risk of being compromised. The immune system does not wire up as it should, there are increases in the risk of anxiety and depression, and our rational thinking and memory are weakened. This is a powerful reminder that we must learn ways to face everyday problems calmly and constructively.

Point 3 – Replace frightened thinking with realistic thinking

Create a THREE STEP "healthy thinking plan" and live by it. This is a great way to take control of problems and difficult situations. To start, you can write the answers asked by the plan below onto paper or to a screen. Over time the steps will become embedded so the idea becomes natural and quick to use.

STEP ONE. Use a catastrophe scale to rate how serious the problem makes a child feel. This helps us to understand the depth of angst they are experiencing.

STEP TWO. Do a risk assessment by working through these questions.

Name the feelings you are experiencing?
What is most likely to happen if you give this a try?
What is the worst that can happen?
What plans can we make, in the unlikely event that the worst happens?

STEP THREE. Do it!

The "Healthy thinking plan" replaces frightened thinking with realistic thinking. By consistently using it, children learn that support is always available, emergency plans can be made, and they can lead a full life. The flip side to this is when fears grow into phobias. This is when a person sets out to deliberately avoid that fear. For example, a child might have a fear of dogs. But it moves to becoming a phobia when this child becomes so avoidant that they avoid seeing dogs, avoid patting dogs, avoid walking on footpaths in case they see a dog, avoid being out the front of their house in case a dog comes by, and avoid fabulous playgrounds, parks, and places worried they might encounter a dog.

Point 4 – Stay active
This can be through organised sport or simply walking and talking with someone most days. Physical activity allows the brain to release endorphins, and these make us feel good.

Point 5 – The gut and brain connection
We are beginning to understand that our brain affects our gut health, and our gut affects brain health. There are now strong links between a balanced diet full of vegetables, protein, and nutrients and good mental health. There is no specific diet proven to relieve depression, although there is mounting evidence that the Mediterranean diet (consisting of whole foods such as fresh vegetables, legumes, whole grains, fish, eggs, healthy fats, especially olive oil) is associated with decreased symptoms and progression of depression. This diet is in strong contrast to the classic Western diet increasingly linked to a heightened risk of depression and obesity. It includes foods such as fast

food, too much red meat, high-sugar desserts and drinks, refined carbs, processed foods, and elevated levels of fat.

Point 6 – Sleep

Seven to nine hours is about right for adults, but children and teens require nine to ten hours each night. When we consistently fall short of the sleep we need, we create what's called a "sleep deficit." This causes moodiness, saps energy, clouds learning, impairs memory, reduces motivation, and as for strong decision-making and concentration, these fly out the window! Sleep aids the reorganisation of the brain, and it's the best learning tool we'll ever receive. Plus, it is free!

Point 7 – Being morally and spiritually connected

Researchers Charney and Southwick identified that those who show better mental health usually have two things in common (Charney and Southwick, 2012). Firstly, they have a moral compass. They possess a strong sense of "right and wrong," "good and evil," "fair and unfair," "helpful and obstructive," "selfish and generous," and all the shades of grey in between. Is this something you do and coach your children to understand?

Secondly, they live with religious, spiritual, or faith values. In fact, having a deep religious or spiritual connection is the single most powerful force that supports people to recover from upsets, emergencies, and disasters. On this, you don't have to suddenly start going to church because spirituality is all about belief, such as the goodness of family, the love and connection to friends, loyalty, generosity, honesty, or sincerity. An extension of this is when you and the kids discuss, and debate, the BIG questions of life:

What's most important in life?
What's the meaning of life?
What gives meaning to your life?
What makes you happy?
What keeps you going?
Why do you want to grow, learn, and become independent?
What are your dreams in the future?

Point 8 – Cognitive and emotional flexibility

Those who display cognitive and emotional flexibility do so much better from a mental health perspective. This is the ability to look at a situation differently, decide to tackle it in an alternate way, even though it feels out-side of your comfort zone and may not feel entirely fair. We step away from our fixed self to "go with the flow" and see where our best effort takes us!

Point 9 – Kindness and giving to others

A simple act of kindness can make a huge difference to someone's day, week, or life perspective. Equally, our kindness to another has a profound effect on our own mental health because connection and contribution leave us feeling valued and uplifted. The research is clear: when we help another, we are the greatest receiver. So, lead your kids to:

Smile or wave to others, often, when appropriate.
Donate their unwanted belongings to local charities.
Find a way to help a neighbour in need.
Turn their birthday into a "for a good cause party" where you ask each per-son coming along to bring something that can be donated to your child's cause.
Or as a family, pitch in and be charitable towards the environment.

Point 10 – Get lost in flow

Flow is a state of mind in which a person becomes totally absorbed in an activity. During flow, one's self magically peels away and the time flies. Flow is associated with a healthy sense of wellbeing and increased happiness. The truth is flow is available to each of us. It occurs when we are fully engaged with our work, with hobbies, in relationships, out on a bushwalk or enjoy-ing our favourite video game for a time. What's your flow activity? What are each of your children's flow activities?

Point 11 – Help your kids to find inspiring role models

Just as you surround yourself with people who are good, respectful, and nurturing, we must encourage our children to do the same. Once again, Charney and Southwick's (2012) research found those with good mental health and high levels of resilience could quickly name their role models. They frequently said that their beliefs, attitudes, and achievements motivated them. These role models can be sporting stars, elite athletes, or wonderful people in your family – even you! Most of us have interesting or compelling histories. Don't forget to share it!

Point 12 – Build structures and routines to improve security and success

A family routine means arranging what needs to happen in a predictable way. This allows children to feel certain and secure, and when feeling like this, they function as best they can. A routine usually includes what we do, when we do it, and how we do it. Classic family routines, rosters, and schedules involve checklists or simple visuals of:

tasks that go with getting ready in the morning
winding down time after coming home from school
mealtime duties; what time, washing hands and setting the dinner table
when after school activities and sport take place
times assigned to play online games
homework time
relaxing options before bedtime
shower or bath times
things to do as your kids prepare for bed at night
chores; packing and unpacking the dishwasher, helping with the laundry, caring for pets, making beds, and cleaning rooms

Our children and teens rely on us to create these simple patterns to ease the pure chaos that busy lives bring into families.

Point 13 – Face your fears and guide your kids to do the same

Today we understand that when we face our fears, they become less frightening. We say to ourselves, "I'm scared, but I can deal with this and learn from it," or "This is a small test that's going to make me more confident." So, every so often, challenge yourself and challenge your children to give something a go that feels slightly outside that natural comfort zone.

As I mentioned at the outset, we cannot precisely control the condition of our mental health, but there is a lot we can do to safeguard, strengthen, and repair it. Please take these mental health hygiene principles with you! Oh? Did my checklist come close to matching yours?

To finish up, I have a gift for you. It's a pretend kaleidoscope. Take it. Gently twist it, and you'll move from seeing one situation from one point of view, to viewing it in a different, more realistic, and helpful light. The kaleidoscope has the power to offer new perspectives and understandings.

It will remind you that children do not arrive as blank slates. So much is influenced by their genes and early experiences. This combines to determine personality, style, anxieties, fascinations, and individuality. So, differing approaches to coach and guide young people count, but the quality of your communication and your deep appreciation of their innate style carry the most weight.

As an educator, allow the kaleidoscope to remind you that your students do not arrive at school as blank slates either. Professor John Hattie's meta-analysis explains that teachers have little control over what kids bring to school because 50% of their variance in achievement is contributed to by genetics, personality, values from home and background experience – aspects well outside of a teacher's sphere of influence (Hattie, 2009). Yet, a teacher's clever efforts account for about 30% of student variance in achievement. He says that a teacher's role is to engage, connect, and wholeheartedly teach because teachers have enough impact to effect positive changes.

Parenting and teaching share an enormous overlap, so let your ever-changing kaleidoscope remind you that you are more than enough, even after a day when you've been challenged, bruised, and feel utterly exhausted! You are enough because you are beautifully intentioned with enough life experience and heart to help them grow, and heal, into the amazing little humans you want them to be.

Which QUADRANT reflects your PARENTING or TEACHING style?

2

This chapter is very personal. I have designed it around the SOCIAL CONTROL WINDOW, so you can quietly contemplate your parenting or teaching style. I want you to think about why you deal with children in the way you do. When confronted with a tough moment is your usual response more likely to be retaliatory, inattentive, indulgent, or respectful? My goal is to inspire you to grasp what your style really is and deepen your relationship with them, so it thrives. And along the way, I will provide a host of practical ideas and techniques to help you communicate, lead, and manage in optimal ways.

So, what is your parenting or teaching style?

Can you name it?

Can you describe it? What does it look and sound like? How does it feel for others?

Are you a terrier constantly barking at the kids, nipping at their heels, and having to have the last say?

Or do you manage with the patience of a saint?

Are you able to guide young people to take calculated risks, rather than swaddling them in over-protection?

Or do you set out each day with the best of intentions only to stumble, blow up, and become frustrated?

Whatever it is, why do you manage in this way?

And what is your natural disposition when the kids will not listen and take behaviours too far?

Is the place you are working from healthy and sustainable for you, your kids, or your class?

DOI: 10.4324/9781003346715-2

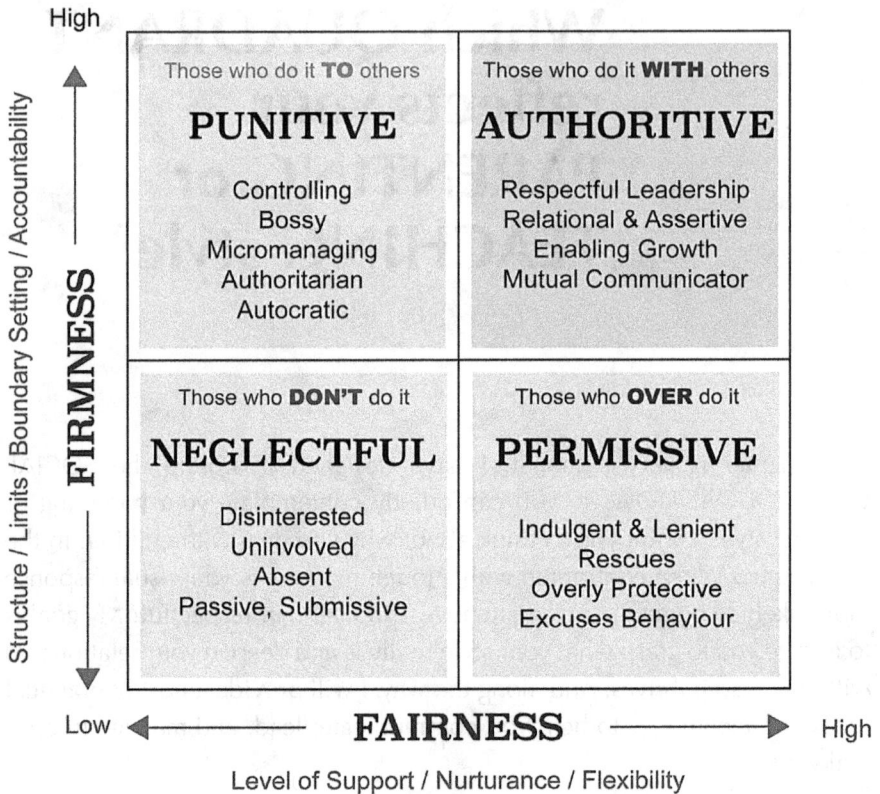

Figure 2.1 The SOCIAL CONTROL WINDOW
Adapted from Wachtel and McCold (2001)

The SOCIAL CONTROL WINDOW is a helpful framework to help us examine our leadership style – how we work with others, how we use our authority and what our style really looks and feels like to others.

As you can see, the SOCIAL CONTROL WINDOW generates four broad leadership styles.

1. The PUNITIVE QUADRANT – for those who dominate OVER children by sharply and aggressively applying limits and boundaries. They control kids in forceful, wordy, and emotional ways, usually in the name of love, care, or safety.
2. The NEGLECTFUL QUADRANT – for those who DON'T do much at all. They are unavailable, disconnected, do not participate much, and let a lot slide by.

3. The PERMISSIVE QUADRANT – for those who OVER do it, OVER justify and OVER nurture. Then suddenly, they get fed up with the high-level input, snap, and jump into the PUNITIVE QUADRANT for a short while.
4. The AUTHORITATIVE QUADRANT (opposite meaning to authoritarian) – for those who are relational, mutual, and kind, but can calmly switch to lead decisively when needed.

I know what you are thinking. You are thinking that on a bad morning, you can jump between each of the four quadrants multiple times! While this may be true, most of us can identify a quadrant we tend to "live in" or "grav- itate to." As well, there will be a quadrant you likely "jump to" when the going gets tough with your kids or students. This is our "default quadrant."

Now is the moment to shine the spotlight on you

In the beginning, as you prepared for parenthood, or "teachinghood," it probably felt like the natural decision to make. What about as a parent? Do you remember? You loved them, they loved you, you could see a future together, and it was divine. As well, your friends were coupling up and some started to have babies. Your parents began to ask about the pitter-patter of lit- tle feet, not to mention the ticking of the unmentionable reproductive clocks in both of you. Yes, having kids seemed a natural next step.

Then, a few short years into having your own children a whole new real- ity dawns. It was a reality that you did not predict, and nor would you have believed it if someone had told you back then. It is what our kids do to us. And they do this thing so much better than anyone else on the planet. They hit our most concealed buttons! Buttons that we guard from the rest of the world. They repeatedly press them and force us to confront our frailties, our quick temper, bad temper, anxieties, fears, dreams, hopes, and lost opportu- nities. There are two ways most adults deal with this. One way is to look inside ourselves and make gentle course corrections over time. Alternatively, we can blame the kids. In this space we invest in the excuse that it is their fault, and they make us all too serious, heated, and wordy.

Years later, a few of us realise we projected the anxieties we held, or the disappointments we experienced, onto our children, notably our first born. Oh, yes – being a parent is a human being's greatest test and greatest joy. It is from being a parent that we learn so much about ourselves if we are open to the learning. In my work, I have seen parents liberated and healed through their own parenting experience. In essence, they take the opportunity to parent their children, grow together, and emulate how they wished childhood had been for them.

In the words of my wise friend, and the initial copy editor of this book, Vanessa…

Children – the great unlockers of life's mysteries. Want to understand your parents? Then become one. Want to relive your childhood? Then be invested in another's. Want to figure yourself out? Then, look in the mirrors offered up by your own kids. Want to learn about unconditional love? It's the fast train on a long, long journey.

Dispelling a myth

As we turn our attention to PARENTING and TEACHING from the AUTHORITATIVE QUADRANT, I must explain the elusiveness of this quadrant. Parents and educators who truly lead within this quadrant bring positivity, empathy, and teamwork to the family and classroom, even in the tough moments. They are connected and emotionally steady. They can seamlessly switch to being delightfully decisive and firm when they need to be. But be warned – this is the quadrant we all aspire to work from. However, the degree of difficulty to consistently manage our young only using the tools from this quadrant is extremely challenging. Can we agree on an important fact? It is, while we aspire to work from this quadrant, we are unlikely to spend 24 hours a day, 7 days a week throughout the year within it.

So, please make me a promise. As you read what follows do not to be too hard on yourself. Resist interpreting each quadrant as good or bad. They simply exist so we can better understand our leadership style. You see, our PARENTING and TEACHING style is not necessarily what we think it is. More to the point, it is how our children, students, colleagues, partners, extended family members, and friends experience our style. This is less about our finest intentions and has so much more to do with how our instincts kick in and spontaneous emotions play out. Please use this time for personal reflection because there is always room for a little improvement within each of us.

THE SOCIAL CONTROL WINDOW – The PUNITIVE QUADRANT

As a parent or educator living in the PUNITIVE QUADRANT, you offer a high level of firmness but low levels of fairness. You create the rules, and maintain them through your sharp words, nagging, criticism, and control. Your children or students do not see you displaying empathy towards them often enough, which is the very ingredient needed to build relationships, loyalty, trust, and connection. As soon as they stray, and "MIS"behave (see Chapter 3 for a reveal on "MIS"behaviour), you overuse your power. Very quickly, to make a point, you withdraw privileges or apply rules. Unfortunately, the tools you are selecting are usually linked to retaliation and punishment which is actually a consequence of your own frustration.

You are a good person, but to you, strength within leadership means you must hold the power, always. You must be the boss, and the ruler who always has the final say – "The buck stops with you!" You rationalise this because you are the teacher backed by a system. And you did well at school. You got the right grades in high school, worked hard at university, and got your degrees. You believe in the old saying, "Don't give students an inch until Easter." Then, little changes after Easter.

The heartbreaking deficit of this style of leadership has not dawned on you. Your tight control, at home or at school, does not offer opportunities for children and teens to practice independent decision making and feel a natural sense of growth, autonomy, and self-assurance. Sometimes you sense disapproval from your partner, friends, or colleagues about the way you manage, speak, and control, but you justify your technique by saying to yourself they are not as deeply committed to the children as you are. This distorted view of commitment sees you constantly manipulating young people, so you remain in control.

When things do not go so well (just as they do not go so well for all of us sometimes), you puff yourself up and trot out confronting threats: "you must," "you will," "don't you dare question me," "I want that now," "how many times do I have to ask," "get to your bedroom," "get out of my classroom," "if you make me ask one more time…" and "don't you dare look at me like that!" Interestingly, you get annoyed with your children and students so much faster than you do with your friend's children. In fact, their children see you as safe, dependable, and fun. How does that work?

Inevitably, when you hit the red or danger zone you immediately think in black and white, in absolute terms, where you must win, and your children or students must lose. And, as you act out your indignant behaviour, yet again you forfeit your relationship with the kids. Your attention is consumed by what went wrong, finding the culprit and letting them feel your disapproval. Your go-to consequences are shouting, belittling, withdrawing things, applying rules, and removing your fondness.

"It's tough to escape the past!"

This reminds me of a recent grumble from an assistant principal of a secondary school. She is a delightful person. During our conversation she said, *"Mark, the Saturday morning detention system is no longer a viable option for students."*

"Halleluiah," I thought to myself. *"Someone who wants to do better than what we did in the past, before we discovered better."*

I adore the concept of trialling new, positive ways to work with students to take ownership for their emotion and behaviour.

Before I could pay my compliment, she continued…

> *"Our detention system is overwhelmed. We encourage teachers to use it. Now the problem is that teachers can't send a student for a Saturday detention in the same week. The system is so backed up that there's a three week wait to get them in!"*

The result of parents or educators working in the PUNITIVE QUADRANT is to teach young people to fight, bite, and run – only to repeat the same misplaced behaviours next time. Your punishing consequences fail to teach them the humane skills to repair the damage they may have caused, and how to re-establish relationships by showing a little empathy and being gentle in the face of tension. Sadly, those who handle young people from this tight, controlling quadrant use tools that are likely to trigger rogue behaviours. Behaviours that are out of character, extreme, and are a consequence of too much control. It does not take long for these young human beings to begin to use the very same tools their parents and teachers have used to control them. They have been taught by experts and the battle is on! As well, a point usually emerges where young teens begin to seek fabulous entertainment by pressing their parents' or teachers' punitive buttons. Here I must share Will's story with you.

Will's story: "We pick an easy target"

I adored working with 17-year-old Will and had done so throughout high school. He was such a character – lively, feisty, friendly, eternally optimistic, and always ready to make a wrong into a right or an injustice into a justice. This meant Will was involved in everything at breakneck speeds, so keeping pace with school assignments was problematic. He was bright enough and happy to do the work. The real challenge was planning, staying organised, sticking with tasks, and reaching deadlines. This was, of course, a consequence of his ADHD identification.

Will walked into my room and plunged his hand into his pocket.

"Take a look at this, Mark. I won it!"

He pulled $140 from his pocket and waved it about, beaming.

"How did you win?" I asked.

"So, we play a game every few weeks at school. Today there were 14 of us and we each put in $10. We pick an easy target. A teacher that always gets cranky quickly and sends kids out of the classroom. One of us is chosen by the group to annoy the teacher with the aim of being sent from the classroom. Each of us pick how many minutes and seconds it will take for the teacher to say, "Get out!"

to the nominated person. And Mark, I won. I guessed 4 minutes and 12 seconds!"

I smiled and replied, "But why choose this teacher?"

Will's response,

"Well, we can't choose a teacher who we like, who likes us, who shares their stuff with us, and is nice. All we're left with are the easy targets. Teachers who don't want to be with us, don't try to like us and have anger problems themselves."

What we are witnessing is a new reality. It is that young people today demand affection within relationships from every adult involved in their life. And in a bid to connect, they will push buttons to experience the full gamut of emotion so they can decide whether to 'tap in' or 'tap out'.

When they 'tap in' they become closer to us, even our supporters. When they 'tap out', they are more likely to see us as the opposition and show this through distant or tricky behaviours.

On balance, children and adolescents will no longer stand to be manipulated by punitive control measures. Their confrontational and antagonistic responses to injustice and unkindness tell us this. We need to grasp that we are witnessing a changing of the guard from one generation of children to another. This generation will not deliver obedience for the sake of obedience. They are shouting from the rooftops, "Nothing positive occurs without relationship and respect." And when they cannot find relationship and respect with significant adults, we see them connecting to others who feel the same way. They are pushed to connect to "that group," "gangs" and shadow groups who also live on the edge because they feel marginalised. Just spend time in some of our primary and secondary schools and watch this playing out. Oh, the world has changed! There is such pressure on us to take stock, to adapt, to reinvent antiquated thinking and outmoded techniques.

THE SOCIAL CONTROL WINDOW – The NEGLECTFUL QUADRANT

In this place, you offer little support and guidance. The adjectives to describe the style include being lax, thoughtless, remiss, careless, indifferent, uninterested, disconnected, selfish, forgetful, and removed. Nothing much is happening between you and the kids. You are unavailable to give them the connection, care, coaching, and guidance that your children or students in your class depend on.

As a teacher, when you look around your classroom you see too many kids, with too many problems. You know what many of them are doing! They are playing video games on their laptops, texting, or watching a screen hidden under their desk, but you turn a blind eye. There are, of course, important reasons motivating your neglectful style. You may have walked into this school and realised, all too late, that it is filled with difficult students and an arrogant leadership. Now, to survive, you have cultivated a chilled, removed approach where you ask for very little. The approach works because it avoids conflict. This soulless space you find yourself in simply allows you to survive!

If questioned about the behaviour of these students, you reply, "What can I do given the backgrounds these kids come from?" Or "What do you expect, we have too many students with special needs."

Please avoid taking the moral high ground here because this is a plea for help. Those stuck in this quadrant, parents or educators, are often struggling with poor health, dealing with the sickness of a dear friend or family member, may be wrestling with a dreadful relationship or relationship breakdown, a separation, alcohol abuse, substance addictions, or a variety of mental health conditions, namely sadness, loneliness, or depression. Perhaps they are overwhelmed by seemingly impossible financial pressures. The truth about life is that it is not as straightforward as we wish it to be.

Perhaps you feel disconnected from your children because you have discovered parenting to be so much less satisfying than you anticipated. If you feel this way, I want to reassure you that you are far from alone. Adjustments can be made and it can become so much better. I have supported many parents over the years who have felt this and carried such heavy burdens of guilt and shame, particularly mothers. If you find yourself in this space, please try to accept it for what it is. This is not about anyone being bad or less. It is the recognition that being a mother, a father, or other parental figure does not always hit the expected highpoints.

Sometimes, we are triggered by memories of our own childhood, and these can cause feelings of inadequacy, turmoil, disappointment, or anxiety. Without knowing it these feelings insert themselves into our relationships with our children and actively oppose the very things we want to build and dream of. There are solutions. We can more easily spot reactions to triggers when we look out for cycles; things happening over and over delivering the same outcome with the same out-of-control feelings. Put the brakes on and respond, rather than automatically reacting. By doing this, we recognise our emotions. Then we move on to rationally think about the next step.

I have also watched parents generate some creative solutions that have made a world of difference. Some, for example, extend their working hours or interests outside the family. They make a commitment to spend less time with their children but improve the quality of the time spent together. I have witnessed this as a real win/win. The result is happier children because they are with a happier parent who wants to be connected.

Have you jumped to the moral high ground, again? Are you thinking there is no way you could ever fit into this neglectful quadrant? Not so. I think we have all been in this quadrant from time to time – for minutes, days, weeks, or longer. There is no judgement here.

When we are in this neglectful zone, we discount the value of searching for and trialling new skills. The determination to plant positive seeds in timely moments with our children vanishes. We forget to encourage, praise, and chase the goals we set together. My heartfelt plea to anyone who feels stuck in this quadrant for too long is to be kind to yourself, and reach out for help from trusted friends, someone within your family or from your GP. If you are the trusted friend someone reaches out to, they will be lucky, because readers of this book either have a compassionate gene or a beautiful empathic quality. Let them know they no longer must pretend everything is alright. Real life is that it is okay to struggle, okay to feel overwhelmed and okay to be supported and find alternatives. Reassure them they can climb from the depths of despair, bit by bit, with a trusting team of their choice around them. I am filled with optimism about this, as I have seen so many adjust and turn this around.

THE SOCIAL CONTROL WINDOW – The PERMISSIVE QUADRANT

Adjectives to best describe the management traits from this quadrant include being too free and easy, free-range, too liberal, laissez-faire, too tolerant, too indulgent, and unlikely to say "no" when it is necessary.

If you work in this quadrant you do a lot right.

You offer loads of time, care, support, and encouragement. However, you struggle to set up and maintain common-sense structures, boundaries, routines, and expectations. Instead, as a parent or teacher, you fluff about serving up a "popular," or an "overly-friendshippy" style. After all, you want your kids or students to be happy, and preferably all the time. You have replaced "relationship and leadership" with a "best friends forever" concept. When chatting to your kids or students you try to use their language and style so they can better relate to you as their confidant. On this, I have had many conversations with teens over the years who feel resentful by the way their parents, teachers, school counsellors, and so on have adopted their generation's language. The consensus among teens is that the adults have their own language style, and they feel more secure when the adults use it.

Working in the permissive quadrant you know your style can be problematic, but you are reassured by the deep compassion you show. As a teacher you make it your business to understand the needs of the students you work with, especially those who face injustices, disadvantage, disability, or trauma-based histories. Unfortunately, your compassion tends to cloud your judgement, and this sees you in conflict with colleagues every so often. Their perception is that you are, yet again, making excuses and will not let young people own their blunders and learn from their mistakes.

Likewise, as a parent, you are your child's most fervent supporter, and heaven help anyone who challenges or holds them accountable for their behaviour because they must deal with you – whether it be another parent, a teacher, the school principal, a relative, or a dear, dear well-meaning friend. And, when your child has a difficulty with a teacher or another child, you are quick to find fault in that teacher, the other child, or their family. You work hard to shield your children from learning through their own hardships, even though you know this process is so very necessary. In fact, you insist that teachers at your child's school make their day filled with fun and happiness, an impossible and unwise ask. You cannot accept that their resilience will grow from a variety of experiences, and that these experiences must include challenge, success, and achievement, but also the experiences of boredom, disappointment, disapproval, sadness, even regret. You carry a "faulty logic" on this, and it gets in the way of your clear-headed thinking and capacity to lead superbly decisively.

Interestingly, you do notice the way your kids consistently push at the boundaries, and you find it annoying and somewhat disrespectful. Your way to tackle this is to use humour and distraction to diffuse it. But it bothers you because this is not what a best friend does to another. Thoughtlessly, you talk to friends and place posts on social media about your own children being especially "spirited." You say that there are two types of kids, the "calm, compliant ones" the lucky parents get, and then there are kids like yours, the "spirited ones." You say, it is just luck of the draw! Your friends, on the other hand, know that there is much more to this equation but say nothing to protect your dignity and friendship.

That one real source of frustration – *the kids pushing at the boundaries to get their way* – is ever present. But you have not yet grasped why they push like this. It is not a personal assault. All children and teens push to work out where our boundaries lie. It is what they must do to feel secure. They need to hear you say "no," over and over, to work out where the limits are. This is a vital dance to help them feel safe and protected; it is all a part of belonging, attaching, and learning how to fit in and accept change. Yet your "faulty logic" shouts if you say "no" you will lose your children's friendship, that you will have to put up with their anger, that you do not want to crush their spirit or that your kids should have everything they want. Sometimes, when there is no way out, you are forced to say "no," but it doesn't really mean "no" because if the kids beg, scream, cry, and threaten they will get what they want. The slipperiness of this slope cannot be overstated. Learning how to deal with not getting exactly what you want is an essential skill that every child needs to experience so they can respond aptly to "no's" and obstacles in adulthood.

Rarely saying "no" comes at a cost. Instead of drawing a line in the sand earlier on by saying "no" you allow your frustration to build. Then later over a seemingly minor issue you snap and you turn into a raging PUNITIVE adult. Unbelievably you jump from the PERMISSIVE QUADRANT into the PUNITIVE QUADRANT, the very quadrant you loathe! Your mouth runs away from you and for a time, the words are threatening and revengeful. You suddenly find yourself taking their phone, laptop, iPad, and every available screen away for days, even weeks! Oh yes, you have grabbed hold of the tools from the PUNITIVE QUADRANT and become too severe in an over-reactive moment.

Once your anger settles, your remorse quickly sets in. Your guilt is inspired by your natural kindness. You now know that you acted too quickly and said too many damaging comments. Soon, you begin to deliver an exaggerated explanation and apology for your overblown actions. Basically, you suck up to your children, and convince yourself that what you are doing is highly poised and empathic. You convince yourself that good parents model apologies and that is all you are doing. But there is much more at play here and it has nothing to do with emotional steadiness and leadership.

The next morning, as a parent, you find yourself preparing bacon and eggs, French toast, and a favourite smoothie for your kids to restore face and bury your indiscretions that are still weighing heavily on you. What have we learned about kids exposed to too much of this emotionally swinging circumstance? This style of management, in more extreme forms, is downright confusing for kids. Sometimes they are the "golden child" and suddenly they are the "black sheep." They tend to lose their place, their confidence, their sense of who they are and what they are capable of. And, if this makes you feel a little uncomfortable or bruised, please be reassured that you are in good company. So many of us exhibit this swinging pattern, jumping between the PERMISSIVE and PUNITIVE quadrants. The trick is to recognise it, do not beat yourself up, and just make small adjustments as you can.

"You don't want to make mummy feel sad, do you?"

Permissive parenting tends to have this feeling, "Oh? Don't talk to mummy like that. You don't want to make mummy feel sad, do you?" says a parent using a frail victim's voice to their stroppy nine-year-old. This is their attempt to appeal to their child's better judgement or nature. But what this empathetic adult has forgotten is that their child's better judgement, just in this moment, has deserted them.

How would you have responded?

Perhaps, this is the time to galvanise a little strength and poise, "Hey? I expect you to speak more kindly than that, especially if you want my help. Try asking me again." Does this sit more comfortably? This is an authoritative style of language where a clear statement is chosen rather than an emotionally based question that a child will struggle to answer rationally. The statement is succinct, instructional, and not inflammatory. It also considers that this nine-year-old has lost their way and requires clear and rational support.

THE SOCIAL CONTROL WINDOW – The AUTHORITATIVE QUADRANT

The research supports an authoritative parenting and teaching style (a style that opposes an authoritarian approach) as most effective for leading and coaching children. An authoritative style begins with respectfulness and understanding that a young person's quest for autonomy is natural, normal, and needed. This is where you lead by showing respect, especially in moments when your child, or a student, displays disrespectful behaviours. You model leadership through your emotional poise and strength, just as you are likely to do with your best friend's children. You are relational, collaborative, emotionally reliable, trusting, and connected. You can, however, effortlessly switch to being pleasantly decisive when you need to be.

You read your kids and students well because you are actively involved in their lives. You make time to be together, you encourage conversations with them. You know their latest interests, joys, fears, friends, and arch-rivals. You progressively absorb how they feel about a range of things. You encourage the sharing of thoughts, feelings, concerns, and questions always without the fear of judgement, humiliation, or embarrassment. While you value honest communication and expect cooperative behaviour, you also know that children and teens will not always get it right.

When they make mistakes, you try to understand the emotional triggers and what might be lying beneath the tricky behaviour. You follow up, privately, to create that special space where we walk alongside them, offering just enough guidance as it is needed, because our best work is always done inside relationships with kids. You subscribe to the adage, "Fewer kindly placed words are more powerful than tell-offs."

Stef's big night out

Stef was just 16 years old and had made an impulsive and unwise decision. He'd had a big night out with his friends and decided to drink six cans of beer in a very short space of time. He was soundly inebriated, and it was too much for his young system. He suffered bouts of dizziness and vomiting with remnants of his stomach contents stuck to his clothing. Then came the time for him to return home.

His friends walked him home and took him to his front door. They responsibly pushed him inside, locked the door behind him and made their getaway. His parent's bedroom light went on and his mum called out, "Proud of you. You're home earlier than you said. Did you have a good night?"

Stef called back, "I'm okay. But you won't be proud of me."

His parents got up and sat with him. Stef told them the story. There was no drama. No lectures. No "I told you so." No disapproval. No retribution. No consequences. His parent's focus was where it had always been; centred on truth, connection, and safety.

"We love you. The most important thing is that you're safe."
"We agree. Your choice was poor, and you suffered the consequences."
"I'll run the shower and we'll worry about your clothes in the morning."
"Let's talk about life lessons tomorrow."

And the statements above reveal why Stef had chosen to share, rather than to conceal it. This scenario serves as a wonderful example of how to guide a young person through a tough moment. His parents remained beautifully composed and built a space where Stef could keep his dignity and be freed from shame. They cleverly left him to own what he'd done, to feel a little remorse and learn something from the unfortunate experience, rather than feeling judged, criticised, and forced into making amends and changes.

As an authoritative leader you continue to learn the cherished language of assertiveness. This is an elusive spot that exists somewhere between being too forceful and too passive. Here the goal is to navigate a way forward and to find a solution. On the one hand, you can respectfully express your own position. You may use language that is frank, but disarming, and maintains the dignity of the other. As well, you appreciate that the harder conversations are never won or lost in a moment. That they are about appreciating each other's position and considerately finding a middle-ground, just as you might do with adults at work. You also appreciate that many issues are not solved in "one sitting," and nor do they have to be.

When the intention is to be assertive, our language highlights the relational language patterns. Notice the use of "I" and "we" and "us" and "our" in the statements and questions below. This language acknowledges feelings and a willingness to improve the situation, and gives hope!

> "'I' want to help."
> "What can 'I' do?"
> "How can 'we' make this better?"
> "'I' agree, it's not fair."
> "Tell me what 'I' can do to make this work?"
> "What can 'we' do to fix this?"
> "'I' overreacted. Can you help 'us' to make this better?"
> "'I' feel the same way as you. What can 'we' do?"

As we reframe our comments to a more productive communication style, we deliberately choose not to get caught up in the drama. Instead, we talk to the "situation." Our focus is on how to achieve an outcome that may even strengthen our relationship. We give a personal connection and a sense that we are in this together.

41

You also understand the deep value of your kids and students feeling connected and attached to you (Firestone, 2015). As they attach to you, they will also feel more inclined to confidently venture into the world and attach to others. Securely attached kids learn a positive world view. They view future relationships as enjoyable and rewarding. Insecurely attached children learn a negative world view. They view future relationships as doomed to fail, problematic, or threatening.

Building attachment is more a mindset, not so much a technique. I can, nevertheless, give you some pointers around how attachment is inspired. Attachment comes from a shared intention involving love, acceptance, security, playfulness, affection, and time. It is curious and empathic; a dance that an emotionally healthy adult and child do together. For some, the connection is built through shared interests, respecting personal space, and learning how best to communicate with them so that they feel safe and heard. It is not a one-size-fits-all and it is up to us to learn what works best and put it into practice. The dance is choreographed by the dancers. It occurs with humour, gentle teasing, kindness, and surprise. We do it with babies, children, and with teens, even older teens. It is contained in the beautifully crafted silly songs, sayings, and statements we repetitively make:

> *"Great to see you again!"*
> *"My love for you is like an elastic band. No matter how far you go, we stay connected."*
> *"I love you stronger than iron and softer than feathers."*
> *"My love for you stretches around the world over and over, to infinity."*
> *"If my love for you had a colour, it would be the whole rainbow."*
> *"The world is a better place because you live in it!"*
> *"I'm happy you're in my class!"*
> *"I like you."*
> *"I'm proud of you."*
> *"That was thoughtful of you."*
> *"You make me smile."*
> *"You were right!"*

These repetitive songs, sayings, and statements bring our kids, and students, closer to us and build precious attachment. Relating in an attached way does not mean being lenient and permissive. Nor does it mean we enjoy the good moments with our kids, but emotionally switch off from them in the tough times. An attachment mindset is all about increasing our emotional availability so our children perceive their needs can be met. There is a lot of scope to get this right. The end goal is that through being attached you will teach skills in an atmosphere of you believing in them. And, over time, you will then set them free to be their own connected person who is healthy enough to attach to others in all kinds of ways.

SOCIAL CONTROL WINDOW – in REVIEW

I hope that by visiting each of the four QUADRANTS you have gained a clearer picture of your leadership style, and how you might tweak it going forwards.

Can you now name the QUADRANT you tend to "live" in?
Are you comfortable with this?
Do you know why you live in it?
Did you inherit it, fall into it, or choose it? Why? What is your story?
Now you know more about the AUTHORITATIVE QUADRANT, might you spend more time in it?
Do you know the quadrant you tend to easily default to when the kids, or situations with students at school, get tricky?
Is the window you are working from emotionally healthy and sustainable?
Do you now have an inkling of other choices available to you?

Most researchers agree that there are clear links between each of the leadership styles and the influence they have on children's thinking and future behaviours. Some suggest the consequences are so strong that they will define a child's behaviour for a long, long time, well into adulthood.

Generally, PUNITIVE, or authoritarian styles, result in children who rank lower in happiness, social competence, and self-esteem, while AUTHORITATIVE styles tend to generate children who are happier and feel more capable and independent. On the other hand, a PERMISSIVE style tends to cause children to rank low in happiness and in the capacity to self-regulate. There is evidence that these children are more likely to experience problems with authority and tend to perform less well at school. The NEGLECTFUL parenting style ranks the lowest across all life areas. These children are more likely to lack self-control, have low self-esteem, and feel less competent than their peers (Sanvictores and Mendez, 2021).

However, do not overlook other contributing factors that shape a child's style, thinking, and behaviours. These influences include cultural dispositions, a child's temperament and personality, and environmental aspects such as the quality of family, peer, and wider community relationships. I'm often asked if parents must be on the same page with their style. In other words, if one parent displays an AUTHORITATIVE style should the other do the same, especially if it is not their natural style? My answer is that it is essential to parent using one's own personality and that children adapt to each of their parent's personal approaches providing they sit somewhere on the AUTHORITATIVE continuum. When children must cope with distinctly different styles, mixed signals can lead to confusion.

The next step is to back yourself and apply some of this learning, gradually. You are a work in progress too. Take small steps, aim for modest improvements, just bit by bit. In summary:

- Kids need to be taught new skills so they can develop new, more functional, and healthy behaviours. Some kids will take longer.
- Focus on progress rather than perfection.
- Your best investment is your enthusiasm.
- Catch the behaviours you value, because praise is THE best tool when it comes to shaping and reshaping the behaviours you want.
- Never go on and on at your kids in heated moments – the window for learning in this moment is non-existent.
- When there is a problem the conversation must be about what happened and how to repair it, never personal, revengeful, or punishing.
- Keep a realistic balance between cleverly guiding your child and being too critical, or judgemental.
- Keep your eye on the main prize – an honest, loving, and enabling relationship.

So, the next time the going gets tough, ask yourself...

"Which QUADRANT am I in right now?"
"Is this most likely to result in a positive solution, and does it have the best chance of strengthening our relationship?"

If not, you know where to move to and which tools to pick up. Your best effort is always enough.

3   "MIS"behaviour

The beginning is to define behaviour. To do this, I want to walk in the garden with you. And while walking, can we chat about the difference between better behaviour and misbehaviour?

Simply put, behaviour is the way in which one acts, or responds, to situations and towards others. Sometimes it is chosen, purposeful, and wise, and at other times it is impulsive, unplanned, or naïve. There's a persistent view that good behaviour is at one end of a spectrum and misbehaviour sits at the other. I am not convinced that they are opposites, nor is what drives them. Behaviour is so much more intricate. Better behaviour embraces mannerisms and responses aligned to acceptable social norms. On the other hand, misbehaviour is a style seen as inappropriate, insensitive, incorrect, different, unexpected, or unwanted.

Let's get back to the garden.

Many of us adore buying a new batch of plants from the garden centre. I do. They come with a description and a planting guide so we know what to do and how they should perform. They have been propagated to fit the gardening norms and will grow predictably and reliably. They will meet our expectations, fill our hearts with joy, and deliver what was promised.

Then there are the less desirable plants. The weeds. They spring up in our garden as a new season begins. They grow fast and chaotically, and their spirit is resolute. Yet a weed can also be a striking plant with wonderful potential. But their random nature makes them an awkward fit in our artificially planned garden design. They can be unsettling. They upset the good order of the plants we have bought and strategically placed.

Do you know the difference between a weed and a desirable plant?

DOI: 10.4324/9781003346715-3

As it turns out, there is not much. And sometimes, there is no easy way to tell. A good gardener will tell you to put away the herbicide and avoid heavy handedness. A good gardener will tell you to leave anything you are not sure about. Get to know it, build a relationship with it, learn about it, ask about it, and wait until it gets big enough, or flowers, so you can understand it! A good gardener will tell you to get down in amongst your plants and weeds because each of them possesses potential.

Weeds do require your thoughtfulness. In the wrong environment, with just a little neglect or mishandling they appear as a pesky problem to be removed and eradicated. Yet the same plant, when nurtured, can grow, blossom, and mature beautifully in the garden. It can even leave us with unexpected memories that touch our souls forever.

This is the moment to declare my position on the term misbehaviour.

I reject it.

This is because it is a negative, one-dimensional concept and does not steer us to think about what motivated the behaviour in the first place. It does not invite us to examine what is happening in our child or teen's world, and how we might subtly and cleverly minimise the stressors. The term misbehaviour embraces punishment and control without understanding. It dupes adults to accept behaviour as an act, often defiant, that is always deliberately chosen.

Hindsight, and a lot of anguish over mistakes made, have taught us that our traditional disciplinary responses to children with trickier behaviours amplified their behaviour challenges. Our POWER-OVER responses reinforced patterns of toxic stress and trauma for them. Without offering our emotional safety and teaching new skills to reshape this "mis"fire it wires up neurologically and deepens. Especially when we reward it, and reinforce it, with our strong, continual, negative emotional feedback. Let us do away with the traditional power battle!

A change in their behaviour begins in our heart

The aim in this chapter is to immerse you in a compassionate way to think about our children's trickier behaviours because behaviour always expresses an underlying emotional need. To do this we use "soft eyes and warm hearts" (Le Messurier, 2020). This is not a suggestion to go soft, disregard the behaviour, and switch to free-range techniques. This is my call to help you think about our instinctive disciplinary responses to children in the hot and heavy moments. Remember that for a long, long time, parents and teachers were encouraged to use POWER-OVER techniques such as strong criticism, harsh words, and punishment as the mainstay to control children. To some degree this remains hard-wired in our minds and egos. A change in their behaviour begins in our heart. So, the next time your child, or any child, says to you, *"Who is the naughtiest kid you know?"* your answer can be: *"Every child's behaviour is communicating a need, and the adults must work out what the behaviour is saying and how to meet that need."*

This mindset directs our thinking from being annoyed by a child's behaviour and urgently over-correcting it, to imagining what is happening for them and how best to humanely meet the emotional need they are expressing. So, the next time your child's emotions are addled, ask yourself:

How are they feeling? Name the emotions they are likely experiencing.

What are they wanting from you? What might fix it? Is this a possible or rational solution?

Is their behaviour likely the result of hunger, thirst, overexcitement, or fatigue?

Are they fearful or anxious and seeking to protect themselves from bullying, failure, or guilt over a misdeed?

Are they trying to connect or be recognised as worthy?

Or is this behaviour purely an impulsive childish act? How do you recognise this?

Or is their response a misguided one based on a "misunderstanding," a "faulty logic," or not being able to see the bigger picture yet?

Or could their clumsy behaviour be inspired by the need for a deeper connection with another person, perhaps with you?

Or is their behaviour inspired by loss. A loss of dignity or a loss of feeling valued?

All behaviour has a purpose although it may not be purposefully directed

Behaviour tells us the purest of stories if we are prepared to switch on, really observe, truly listen, and imagine what it must be like for another in this moment. Behaviour (good, poor, or anywhere in between) is what we

humans do to survive an instant. As adults, we need to be emotionally intelligent and scratch below the surface to work out which emotions are driving
the behaviour, instead of simply responding to the irritation the behaviour
causes. Here are opportunities to practice.

No letting go

ACTIVITY

In this first scenario, imagine you have arrived at the park for an extended
family gathering. Wow, it is much bigger than you anticipated. There are
families everywhere. Finally, you find a place close to those you love and
know. Curiously, your nine-year-old daughter will not leave your side. You
repeatedly ask her to go and play with her cousins. She refuses, will not
speak, and clings tightly to your leg. It is not a good look and you feel somewhat embarrassed. This is most unlike her.

> Firstly, what's likely triggering this kind of behaviour?
> Secondly, name the feelings she is experiencing?

To stretch your thinking, think of your own child or a young person you
know. Then arrange the suggestions below from most likely to least likely:

> *"I had no idea we were coming to this."*
> *"I don't feel safe."*
> *"My cousin hurt me last time."*
> *"I can't do it."*
> *"I'd prefer to be home on my device."*
> *"I need a drink."*
> *"I'm overwhelmed."*
> *"I feel sick."*
> *"I'm too shy to do this."*
> *"There's someone here I don't like."*
> *"You never said it would be like this."*
> *"I didn't get my screen time this morning."*

Next, what can you do right now to ease this?
    Finally, what can you do later so something can be learned from this
tricky moment?

Fast and furious

In this second scenario your 11-year-old son has three friends at home for a sleep over. Two are longstanding close friends, and the other is new to the group. It is 8 pm and they are taking a break before watching another movie. Your boy has been hard to reach all evening, talking over the top of others, loud, and showing off.

Firstly, what's changed your boy's usual behaviour?
Secondly, name the feelings your boy is likely experiencing?

To stretch your thinking, think of your own child or a young person you know. Then arrange the suggestions below from most likely to least likely:

"I've got to impress my new friend."
"I'm carrying a lot of responsibility to be a great host."
"It's harder than I thought. I'm having to do all the talking."
"Do you think I'm being funny enough so the boys will like me?"
"Boys notice me. I'm fun!"
"I'm worn out."
"I'm thirsty."
"This isn't going so well."
"They're not including me."
"Help!"

Next, what can you do right now to ease this?
Finally, what might you do later so something can be learned from this tricky moment?

Coming home from the park

You caught up with two dear friends for a coffee and a chat in the park after school.

The kids played while the three of you were immersed in a compelling conversation. There were five children. Four of them are girls and the one boy is yours! He's nine years, your daughter is eleven years, and the other girls are a little older. After half an hour or so you left the park and headed home. Early on during the drive home your daughter shoots a jibe at your son about his "stupid musical taste" and the way he gets the lyrics in songs mixed up. Instantly he launches himself from the back seat, grabs her neck, and with an open hand hits her hard on the forehead, screaming obscenities at her. Predictably she screams back urging you to save her!

It's this a simple act of unbridled violence? Is what you are witnessing an explosive performance triggered by a backstory?

Firstly, what may have occurred that has set this boy's wild behaviour off?

Secondly, name the feelings this boy is experiencing?

> "They made fun of me the whole time at the park."
> "I love hurting my sister."
> "I was made to feel stupid by them and my sister didn't help me."
> "Take this for what you did to me. You made me embarrassed."
> "I felt bad. See how bad this feels."
> "It's still not even. I'd never do what you did to me!"
> "I'm fed up."

Next, what do you do right now to ease this explosive moment?

Finally, what will you do later so something that is beneficial can be learned from this tricky moment?

Up, up, and away, again!

ACTIVITY

Ruby is in Year 9 and rarely engaged with schoolwork. She needs to be closely managed to get any work completed. She frequently gets up and out of her seat and moves about in class chatting quietly during quiet and focused work time. She's pleasant enough but shows no commitment. Why? What's going on for her?

Firstly, what's possibly behind this girl's disengagement?

Secondly, name the feelings she is likely experiencing?

> "Oh? I've forgotten again. What am I meant to be doing?"
> "Those words. They just float all over that page."
> "Yikes! I can't do the work, again!"
> "I'd rather sit next to…"
> "How is this connected to real life?"

"Notice me because we need to talk."
"You should have seen what happened again at home last night."
"I'm so hungry I could eat a desk."
"I'd rather get your consequence than do this."

Next, what do you do in this moment to help?
Finally, what might you do later to support this girl's emotions and behaviour?

Won't or can't?

Arlo is a Year 7 student. At the moment he's refusing to join in with the class and will not follow your directions. This is most unlike him. Usually, he's easy going, keen to please, and friendly!

Firstly, what might be behind this behaviour? It is most uncharacteristic. Secondly, name the feelings he may be experiencing?

"I don't feel safe in here. I'm being bullied."
"I have to talk to you. This is going to be humiliating."
"I have to talk to you. I can't go home."
"I can't go to my next class because of what happened."
"I got punched and kicked at lunch."
"I'm hot, tired, hungry, thirsty. I'm done."

Next, what do you do in this moment to help him?
Finally, what might you do later to support him and build your connection?

My take on "MIS"behaviour

Throughout this book, from now on, I will use the word misbehaviour deliberately in this way: "MIS"behaviour. Note the emphasis on MIS. In other words, a lot of what we call "MIS"behaviour is due to "MIS"firing, "MIS"cuing, "MIS"understanding, "MIS"adventure, a hiccup, inexperience, exuberance and impulsivity, or the urge to protect or impress. So much of the behaviour we see in young people is simply "MIS"guided and "MIS"placed.

The fact is most children, at every stage of development, will display problematic behaviours. Almost always these are temporary in nature. And, for young people who live complicated lives – those battling disadvantage, disconnection from family, disability, disorders or deficits, and trauma-based histories – we especially need to appreciate how this added dimension stirs "MIS"behaviour. Children in this cohort are vulnerable and genuinely struggle to choose their behaviour. Interestingly, what do you think the leading intervention is, for such children and adolescents? The leading intervention is adults (parents, grandparents, foster parents, and educators in schools) who work to build emotionally safe, steady relationships with them and understand how they have been emotionally impacted by their past. We now understand that emotion and behaviour cannot be separated.

Lessons from the past

In the past our traditional response to "MIS"behaviour was retaliatory and punishing and often veiled as fair. History has taught us that the forces of dominance, punishment, and exclusion frequently amplified a young person's behaviour challenges. Teachers in schools and parents at home entered heated moments with young people carrying a sledgehammer. This heavy handedness reinforced the patterns of toxic stress and trauma in many children. And this is why our thinking has shifted to connection, dignity, and belonging.

There is a shift to accept that children are reliant on our modelling and poise. Many rely on us to defuse situations for them. Without offering our understanding and teaching NEW SKILLS, children are robbed of opportunities to understand, heal, and improve. All of this takes persistence and time.

4   **Understanding the STUBBORNNESS of behaviour**

Never assume that managing another person's behaviour is an easy or predictable thing to do. It is not. Managing our own behaviour is tough enough! Managing someone else's is much harder (DiSalvo, 2017). There is a stubbornness, a persistence and doggedness about behaviour that must be understood. Before we make any attempt at changing the behaviour of another, we must appreciate the essence of this stubbornness.

What about you?

How are you doing in the quest to change a few of your own behaviours?

Have you picked up your exercise routine? Is it going regularly and well? Are you reaching your goals?
Are you eating more healthily more often? Has takeaway become less frequent?
How are your fitness goals tracking?
Are you drinking less alcohol?
How is your quest to cut back on sugar, carbs, gluten, or red meat?
Have you finally got a better balance between work, family, friends, and fun?
Are you spending less time on your phone and worrying about it?
Have you pulled back on the time you were spending on social media?
Are you spending less and saving a little more?
Have you got your credit card debt under control?
You do have your tax return in, don't you?

DOI: 10.4324/9781003346715-4

Changing our own behaviour is hard. But changing the behaviour of another is so much tougher. It is achievable but there are a few conditions that must be acknowledged. Only then we begin to understand why changing behaviour is as tricky as driving into the sun on a long and windy road. It takes time, determination, and a deft style!

Crossed arms

ACTIVITY

Let me explain with this apparently simple activity I have borrowed from my book, *Teaching Values of Being Human* (2020, pp. 226–227). It provides a clear idea of how deeply ingrained "old behaviours" are and how tricky it is to reshape them with new, more functional behaviours.

Please do this. Cross or fold your arms across your chest. Easy, eh?
Now, uncross them. Shake your arms to relax them. Do it again – cross them across your chest.
Now, uncross them and give them another shake to loosen them up.
And for the last time, cross them again!

What did you notice about crossing your arms?
Yes, you crossed them the very same way each time.
The same arm went over the top of the other each time.
And the hand of the lower arm sat on the bicep of the top arm.

Why?
You have likely done it this way for a long, long time, so it has become a habit or behaviour.
It feels comfortable, relaxing, safe, and secure. It is what you know.
It is patterned, ingrained, or fixed. Let us call this your OLD WAY or your OLD BEHAVIOUR.

Next, I want you to cross your arms across your chest, again.
But this time I want you to switch your arm positions so that the one that was on the bottom is now on the top.
Let us call this our NEW WAY or our NEW BEHAVIOUR.

Off you go – cross your arms across your chest the NEW WAY.
Tricky isn't it?

Now, you must really think!

It is much harder to get your arms in the right position and your fingers are
    struggling to feel right.

Suddenly, you have a sparkling and very real insight into the struggle of
letting go of an old, entrenched behaviour, and picking up a new one to
replace it. The NEW WAY took you a while, and with some added thinking
and effort, you got there. But this NEW BEHAVIOUR feels different, uncomfortable, weird, odd, and requires purposeful thought every time you do it!
This makes it so easy to give way and slide back into the comfortable OLD
WAY. And this is our children's struggle as we ask them to switch from an
OLD behaviour to a NEW behaviour.

The traditional negative approach

Are you more likely to stick with the NEW WAY if I keep criticising, nagging, and humiliating you each time you fail to do it? What if I constantly
say, *"Stop it! You're making another B-CHOICE. I saw you do the NEW WAY
before. You can do the NEW WAY when you choose to try! You are choosing
not to cooperate!"* This approach will not help! As my child or student, you
will get annoyed at me, our relationship will become bruised, and you are
likely to sabotage my goal. We also know that continued exposure to critical methods is likely to provoke oppositional behaviours and mental health
issues in developing human beings. What the overuse of tell-offs and repri-
mands does is to train children to self-protect by blaming, lying, minimising,
and disregarding.

A positive approach

Are you more likely to stick to the NEW WAY if we try to get on the same page
together? If we are honest with each other about why the NEW BEHAVIOUR
matters and about the underlying obstacles around behaviour change? What
about if we try to work on it together and chunk the transitions into smaller
parts so we are more likely to find success? What about placing an emphasis
on being collaborative, optimistic, and finding novel ways to celebrate little
achievements along the way? In this space, we set up an approach where we

support each other, prompt each other, and use new encouraging language that helps to see more of this NEW BEHAVIOUR?

Simply put, this is the little known and uncensored backstory about behaviour change. Now you can see why blindly stomping on poor or disappointing behaviour in the name of obedience is so short-sighted. The message to those who have behaved misguidedly or inappropriately is, *"You've acted badly, so now you will be treated like a bad person."*

When a child or teen feels admonished, is made to feel like a bad person, is backed into a corner, and has nothing left to lose, "rogue behaviours" are roused. These are rebellious and defiant behaviours triggered by pure frustration and transform into angry, explosive behaviours or scowling, non-compliant ones. The point here is that the behaviour is out of character and is a response to too much adult control. Too much control is very different to exercising compassionate leadership. Signs of controlling parents and educators usually include:

1. An over-focus on acquiring obedience.
2. Discouraging children's choices and independence.
3. Dictating most aspects of the child's life.
4. Statements such as "because I said so" to control. Thinking they are always right.
5. Withdrawal of affection from children to show disapproval.
6. Frequently use empty threats, criticisms, and shaming.
7. Unrealistically high expectations.
8. Many rigid rules.
9. A lack of give and take, and empathy.
10. Not respecting a young person's privacy.

This is a world away from the message I want you to leave with your kids and students. I want you to leave the message, *"You're fabulous, but that behaviour isn't working. Let's change it up together!"*

Stubbornness: A different perspective

Many of us, adults and children alike, share a character trait called stubbornness. It often expresses itself through a wariness about change, a perceived loss of control, or a sudden loss in pride. Then, in a heartbeat, we can make decisions we later regret. Here is a plea to be sensitive to our own stubbornness, and stubbornness within the personalities of our children. Just as you have felt it, when a child is suddenly pressed to follow an instruction, perform a task, or follow rules they were not expecting and cannot wrap their head around, stubbornness is produced.

Here are a few ideas to help you work with this complicated temperamental trait.

Firstly, recognise that this is part of your child's character. Their response is usually not a conscious response to get at you! Also consider that the positive side of stubbornness is persistence. A valuable life attribute!

Secondly, when they become stubborn respond with poise, bring them closer to you, slow the interaction down, provide options, break the task into smaller pieces, and relieve the pressure to instantly perform. Gradually, teach them skills so they can deal with this trait better in the future.

Thirdly, prioritise issues that deserve your attention. Focus on the current issue. Do not allow your runaway emotion to hurdle jump into the future by saying, "Well if you can't get your head around this now, how bad will it be when you're a teenager!" This kind of talk throws up too many unnecessary complications and is plainly damaging. Of course, when your child responds well, praise them, and state the behaviour that worked!

Finally, consider your own temperament and behaviour. Would it help if you were less stubborn in your child's stubborn moments? When our stubbornness consistently meets theirs, we are likely to inspire oppositional behaviours in our kids.

Behavioural change can only begin when we understand the natural resistance or stubbornness within our personalities, and how this impacts on those we love and care for.

5 | A language that TAMES SHAME

Shame is a learned, deeply self-conscious emotion. We believe it starts around two years of age with the arrival of language and self-image. We understand that to be ashamed of ourselves someone of significance must have put us to shame. Shaming messages are most powerful when they come from those we are closest to – the people we love, admire, or seek recognition from. Therefore, a parent or teacher's shaming are likely to leave the deepest cuts on our young. And, as you might expect, because children are more vulnerable than adults, shaming messages received in childhood are considerably more difficult to erase.

Shame in human beings is triggered following communication that has prioritised rejection, humiliation, intimidation, destructive criticism, or insulting statements to make a point. Rather than addressing the problem, the behaviour, or the situation, the interaction turns personal. In turn, this triggers feelings of disgrace or worthlessness, on a sliding scale of severity. At the upper end of severity, shame inspires opposition, spite, and revenge. And this is why shame is one of our most difficult emotions to cope with.

Messages of shame are usually verbal, but great shame can be carried in a look, such as disdain, contempt, or disgust. The words, voice tone, body, and facial gestures we use in any interaction always signal one of two intentions. They indicate an intention to preserve another's dignity, or an intent to grab power, win, or hurt. As guardians of this precious space, we must teach ourselves to avoid language that encourages "the blame game" where one is elevated to be a winner and the other shamed to be the loser.

DOI: 10.4324/9781003346715-5

Today everyone agrees it is wrong to hit a child to make them do what we want

Surely, it is just as damaging to use words that provoke shame in another, especially in a child or young person. I think so. Yet, shaming is a common control method that has long, long been used to regulate our children's behaviour. Sometimes it is inadvertent. At other times it is used as a deliberate disciplinary tool and to appease our own frustrations. We shame our children and students when we want them to feel small or defeated. There is no blame here because parenting and teaching is an emotionally complex gig with a controlling backstory. My goal is to empower you by building awareness about shame, its prevalence, and repercussions.

Just as we are careful never to shame a treasured friend, we must be equally sensitive never to direct any unkind words at our children, or students, in a heated moment. Such words hold the power to tear away at the innate goodness of a young human being. A careless word or two here and there – well, they happen in the ebb and flow of life, and providing they are welded to a loving and trusting relationship their impact is minimal. But much beyond this, words have the power to mis-shape a child's reality. And to prove this, most of us carry hurtful words we were told as a child, and at certain times, they replay in our mind to undermine our optimism.

Never pretend that shaming is isolated to a certain postcode. It is not. Shaming occurs from the "nicest" of people and within the "loveliest" of environments. Shaming is unacceptable because it sends our children backwards. It has the capacity to change a child's behaviour, negatively, and inspire mental health difficulties characterised by anxiety, opposition, aggression, and timidity.

"You're so stupid!"

I work with a family and have grown close to them. This mother has vivid memories of her father saying, "You're so stupid," in front of guests at her fifth birthday party when she spilt a drink. It has always stuck with her and now when she makes a mistake, or could have done better, her father's voice replays in her mind as, *"I'm so stupid! I'm so stupid!"*

Shaming fails to keep the people we love close to us. Rather than teaching through empathy it demonises another's shortcomings. Shame does not help a person make the connection between their behaviour, doing the best they can, how they can make a change, or acting with care. Shaming can break a young person's spirit and break the precious connection with us. Shaming a child sits squarely on the child abuse spectrum.

There are many huge and horrendous examples of shaming situations. They range from body and racial shaming to gender and public shaming to homophobic and age shaming, and more. The three examples below are deliberately chosen because they are low key and reflect a lot of the action that takes place in our homes and classrooms.

The dance of shame

"Mum? I left my schoolbag at school?" says her 13-year-old son as he remembers his homework too late in the evening.

"Oh, seriously? This is the third time in two weeks, Jack. You'd lose your head if it wasn't screwed on! I may as well burn those school fees for all the good they're doing," Mum remarks.

So, how might mum's response trigger shame in her son? Firstly, it amplifies this boy's personal frustration. He is already feeling annoyed at himself. His Mum has done little wrong, but her comment stirs shameful feelings.

In the instant she said, *"Oh, seriously?"* her questioning tone and eye-roll raised feelings of ridicule and worthlessness in this young man. He had not set out to leave his schoolbag at school. He wished it were different and had his homework in his bag.

This is the beginning of the dance of shame.

Next, Mum said, *"This is the third time in two weeks, Jack. You'd lose your head if it wasn't screwed on!"*

This comment prompted Jack to think, *"Didn't know you were counting. Didn't know you see me as so pathetic and heads aren't screwed on anyway!"*

He swallows these unpleasant feelings and bravely calls out, *"Don't worry Mum I can do it at school before the lesson. It's under control!"*

Trying to be light-hearted mum quips, *"Slap dash gets the job done, but mate, where's the value for my school fees!"*

Now the stage is set for her dear boy to bite back because shame diminishes one's integrity and it feels like there's little to lose. Jack bites back, *"You're always going on that I'm not worth your stupid school fees. You know I don't care. Send me where you like."*

What Mum now hears is that her beautiful boy is rude, and forgetful. For Mum, the exchange has reinforced that she is not getting value for money and her son does not care about his learning.

13-year-old Jack has been reminded that he will never be as good as his older sister. She went to the same school, worked hard, got great grades, and always made her parents proud.

This is how shame heightens emotions and prompts the use of protective strategies designed to keep up the appearance of dignity and pride. We must understand the dance of shame and become expert at using language that does not provoke it. If we are unable to appreciate the dance of shame and our role in changing it, then we should not be surprised to see our children rise to our influence and deliberately push against us.

To finish up, let us replay this scenario in a way that would have diminished the dance of shame and offered help…

"Mum? I left my schoolbag at school?" says her 13-year-old son as he remembers his homework too late in the evening.

"Oh, that's annoying for you. Can I help?"

Can you see the difference? I think you can feel the difference too.

When we are in an ashamed state our feelings become spring loaded. This is called hypervigilance. Hypervigilance is an amped alertness where we are super-sensitive and anxious to our surroundings. In this state our reasonable perception deserts us and the consequence is to overreact to others, and situations, at any given moment. So, when we meet a speedbump or hiccup, that spring, loaded with shame, causes us to catastrophise and unleash big, fast feelings!

Reawakening shame

So, let me tell you about seven-year-old Owen. He is my client and I adore him and his beautiful parents. Owen is a great kid, physical, sporty, speedy, and moral. He throws himself into life, and at his friends, at a hundred miles an hour. It is fair to say that Owen crams 70 minutes into every hour! The

problem is, his style does not give him time to think, time to self-regulate his emotions, and find a little composure. Instead, he tends to crash and burn. And afterwards, Owen is his own worst critic.

I remember seeing him after experiencing an unusual fortnight of high-level emotional and behavioural hiccups. Nothing was going right for Owen. He was reacting and blowing up over the slightest of things. He was truly hypervigilant, and it started when he had lashed out and hit his best friend. Owen's principal and teacher sorted it out at school and helped Owen to repair the damage. I will always remember what his principal said to him. Owen told me because it had stuck with him too. It was, *"Owen? We must talk about when you hit Ti. But before we start, I want you to remember this is one mistake, and it's amongst a lot of great things you do really well most of the time."*

His mum was told what happened and that it had been sorted at school. However, Owen's mother is a good and responsible person and took his "MIS"behaviour at school seriously and personally. Subsequently, she applied consequences at home for his wrongdoing at school. Double-consequencing is rarely a good idea. As well, she lectured endlessly, especially each morning on the drive to school. She would go on and on telling Owen:

"I want you to be good today."
"No hitting YOU can't hit or hurt anyone."
"Dad and I never hit. We don't want YOU hitting."
"Remember, use safe hands."
"And while you're at it, safe feet too!"
"If you choose not to do this, there will be trouble when YOU get home."
"YOU don't want to disappoint dad again tonight do YOU."
"I want YOU to control yourself."
"YOU may not be able to control others, but YOU can control what YOU do."
"YOU can do this. YOU must do this."

Poor Owen. He arrived at school filled with dread, his shame rekindled, and in a hypervigilant state. Then, as soon as a curveball came his way he'd blow up because he felt so hopelessly bad and defeated!

Using shame as a control technique

An email from a friend, who is a leader in a school, follows.

Hi Mark. I must share this with you because I know your head and heart is wired the same as mine. It was the end of the school day and I was sitting quietly, chatting with a student on a fence near the school crossing. With hindsight I now realise we were somewhat concealed from others using the crossing.

Suddenly, the teacher on duty was shouting and agitated! His shouting was directed at a delightful Year 10 student. She is so bright, so kind, and so absent minded. As it turned out, she had her head stuck in a book and followed a group across the road. However, she should have waited. The duty teacher launched into action and proceeded to belittle and shame her in front of the other students. The teacher was well inside her personal space screaming for all to hear, "It's not rocket science, when the light is red it means stop, when its green it means go. What's wrong with YOU?" I caught up with her and asked if she was okay? We chatted and she left feeling reassured. My next job is to counsel this teacher because shaming has no place in good schools. And to be a good teacher, and a decent human being, this teacher needs this learning.

Yet another reminder that shame has long been a foundational method to control our children's behaviour. We must recognise that in our efforts to get children to behave in a way we see fit, we do not damage them. Our talk can be direct and candid, but must never deliberately infuriate them, shrink their self-esteem, inflict hurt, or cause them to doubt their competence or themselves.

Recollection by a parent: When Callum wanted to own it

Recently, when Callum got into trouble at school Mark's comforting words flashed into my mind; breathe, listen, smile at Callum, put your arm around him, pull him closer and tell him you love him no matter how bad it is. Then slowly deal with it together and keep breathing.

I have a responsible role as a social worker but lose my skills and good sense when I'm summoned to the principal's office as a parent. It doesn't help that they won't tell any of the details in that first phone call, so one spends the drive contriving the worst possible scenarios, then, by the time you reach school you're a blithering mess inside.

I arrived. I saw Callum, made eye contact, smiled, stood next to him, pulled him close and softly asked, *"Are you okay?"*

I listened to the deputy recount the unfortunate situation and why it caused such disruption and distress. The boys had clearly made a poor choice. I also listened to the parent of the other boy involved scolding their child in front of everyone. They were trying to be responsible, but how they did it, what they said, and in this moment, was shaming and humiliating for their boy. We accepted the school's consequences. They were strong and fair. Then we left.

In the privacy of our car, I quietly asked Callum what happened. He engaged, which isn't always the way. He could see how things went pear-shaped. He explained that things escalated, and he became shocked and stuck. We were able to brainstorm a couple of safer alternative solutions he could have used. Not many words were used. Then, without prompting he said, *"I'm going to need to work hard to get their trust back."*

I don't want you to think I'm always this calm and insightful when things go wrong. I'm not. On this occasion I channelled a few of the insights I'd gleaned from Mark over the years.

Erin

YOU- and I-statements

So, how do we become better at using language that is honest, kind, and free of judgement? The style of language that builds a space where children can thrive. It starts by exploring the differences between "YOU-statements" and "I-statements."

"YOU-statements" are a damaging language pattern, bound to provoke shame.

"I-statements" belong to a relational language pattern that arouse trust, connection, and resolution.

These provide a practical starting point!

YOU-statements

YOU-statements are provocative. They search for fault, wrong, inadequacy, or blame. Here are the regular shaming culprits.

"YOU naughty boy!"
"YOU'VE been a bad girl."
"What's wrong with YOU?"
"What's YOUR problem this time?"
"Why are YOU doing that?"
"Don't YOU ever think?"
"Why are YOU making me cross again?"
"YOU'RE selfish!"
"How many times do I have to tell YOU?"
"I'm over YOU!"
"Big boys don't cry. YOU need to toughen up!"
"YOU sound like a galah going on like that!"
"Why are YOU making me wait for YOU?"
"YOU never do what you're told."
"I'm fed up with YOU!"
"Why do YOU make mummy sad."
"How many times do I have to tell YOU?"
"Do I need to remind YOU again?"
"None of the other children are acting like YOU are."
"Wish YOU were like your sister."

Can you remember when you were on the receiving end of a "YOU-statement"? What happened? Was your instinct to give back just as good as you got? Or did you go quiet and defensive to protect yourself? Conflict in these moments can escalate super-fast because emotions and the capacity to self-regulate them is under siege. And once embarrassed in this way every well-adjusted individual loses faith in the other, little by little.

To summarise:

YOU-statements shout out who is taking the power, making a conflict inevitable.
YOU-statements make it personal.
YOU-statements generate a winner and loser situation.
YOU-statements do not provide a space for a young person to feel a little guilt, to feel some remorse about what they did, and find a way to make things better.
YOU-statements invite hostile thoughts, flipping out, and aggression.
YOU-statements are destructive.

I-statements

"I-statements" help to create a poised and secure language pattern. Here, the focus is directed towards solving a problem and preserving the self-respect of the other or others. This emotionally healthy pattern of words (and thinking) frequently uses the words, "I," "we," "us," "together," and "our," rather than "YOU."

> *"How can I make this a bit easier?"*
> *"How can I make this better?"*
> *"I can see you're upset. WE love you and can work it out WITH you."*
> *"Just wanted to check. What can I do to help?"*
> *"That didn't work. How can WE fix it?"*
> *"I want to help. What can I do?"*
> *"I agree. I think WE can do better."*
> *"This is about US not YOU. WE can work it out."*
> *"Tell me what I can do to make this work?"*
> *"I've got your back."*
> *"Of course, WE can work it out."*
> *"I don't think I explained it very well. How can I change it?"*
> *"I feel the same way. Let's do this TOGETHER."*

These statements acknowledge feelings and a willingness to immediately improve the situation. They instantly give hope. We use our face, our words, the tone of our words and our body language in a way that will contribute to the best outcome. We consciously let go of language that blames, harms, or inflames. There is a strong chance that this process will strengthen our relationship. We try to truly feel what the other is feeling in this moment. "I" and "we" and "us" statements give a personal connection and a sense that we are in this together, and together, we can find a way forward.

The HOLY GRAIL – healthy communication patterns in the tricky moments

To review, here are ten tips to promote healthy communication and avoid the possibility of shaming. They are wonderfully straightforward. The real trick is to use these straightforward principles in the hot and heavy moments.

1. Keep your feelings in check. It is never about winning or immediately fixing the problem. Respond in the same way you would respond to a dear friend. Place an emphasis on kindness, emotional steadiness, and strength even when their feelings are running wild.
2. Do not justify, defend, or get too wordy. You may have to take control and say, "I want to fix this…" or, "How can we work on this together?"
3. In the first instance, say sorry or agree. "I'm so sorry you're feeling like this. How can I help?" "I agree, this is upsetting…"
4. Ask yourself, "What can I do to be most helpful in this moment?" Connect by using "I-statements" and words such as "I," "we," "us," "together," and "our."
5. Use connecting gestures that indicate you want to, and can, do this together.
6. Validate their feelings. Ask a question. Help them express their feelings. "I can see how you feel…" or "I can see why you feel that…"
7. When you see their emotions surging, slow the interaction down. Help them to gain composure from your composure. The first goal is to be with them. Breathe. Show empathy. Do not look too slick – authenticity is best!
8. The prize is using language that is helpful, not confrontational. If you would not say it, or do it, to someone you admire then do not say it, or do it, to your child or student.
9. If you cannot find a compromise or realise you must draw a line in the sand, then you have two options. Simply state how it must be or review the situation and set a time for a follow-up!
10. The goals – to find a resolution and keep everyone's integrity intact!

Revenge fantasies

Without this understanding about healthy communication patterns, we are far more inclined to stubbornly enter a battle and force young people into obedience. When we do this we never really win, even when we convince ourselves we have won. What happens is that our child or teen or student loses face, and we have inadvertently built an eager opponent, or much worse, a secretive enemy with a festering grudge who is prepared to lay in wait.

On this, consummate Australian educator Ian Lillico once wrote:

> Schools need to review their pastoral care and disciplinary proce-
> dures so that the current pre-occupation with punishment changes to
> natural consequences for misbehaviour. Children who are punished
> often have revenge fantasies that interrupt true remorse for what they
> have done. Girls and boys who are quickly punished by our school
> systems are not given the opportunity to make amends for what they
> have done, as punishment clears the ledger and allows boys to re-
> offend in the future without attendant feelings of guilt.
>
> (Lillico, 2021)

Ever had a revenge fantasy?

ACTIVITY

Have you ever felt so unfairly or harshly treated that there was no learning
from or owning it? That all you wanted to do was to pay that person back? If
so, you are completely normal because when any human being, especially a
child, feels disconnected and shamed we often see an escalation in revengeful behaviours. Numerous studies now link shame with a desire to punish
others. Shamed individuals are more likely to be vindictive, aggressive, or
self-destructive.

I am also compelled to link the idea of children telling lies to feelings of
shame because this is the basis of many conversations I have had with parents and educators.

Lying usually happens when children dig themselves into a hole and
can't see a way out. In this moment they become preoccupied with being
exposed and getting into trouble. Feelings of guilt and disgrace swamp
them. Suddenly a new goal emerges: manipulating the truth to avoid more
trouble.

This is not a sign of a child heading down the slippery slope to wicked-
ness! Rather, it is our call to duty. The best way to help children avoid lying
starts with a little openness and honesty from us.

Reassure them that telling a lie to cover their tracks is not a giant sin, it is
a mistaken logic drawn on to get rid of the problem. Explain they can always
tell the truth because you will make a precious space for the truth to be told
without judging, interrupting, or telling them "I told you so" or worse.
Sometimes, quite inadvertently, good parents and teachers respond to a

child telling lies too assertively and turn such events into battles that must be blatantly won so the alleged liar feels squashed and further shamed.

The mystery of the missing crisps

I recall the creative way Stacey responded to her 11-year-old son, Tyler, who was taking small packets of crisps from the pantry without asking or conceding he was. Stacey, to her credit, stayed calm and offered Tyler all kinds of possibilities to access the crisps without feeling the need to steal or lie. This provided some improvement, but what happened next brought the saga of the missing crisps to a close. Stacey was vacuuming Tyler's room and decided to vacuum under his bed. In this moment, she discovered 27 empty packets of crisps. She finished the vacuuming, took the empty packets into the kitchen, placed them on trays and popped them into the oven to shrink them. Once they were cooled, she returned to Tyler's bedroom, pulled his quilt back, laid all 27 shrunken crisp packets out on his sheet, and gently pulled his quilt back up. Tyler discovered them as he climbed into bed that night. He did not say a word. However, as Stacey kissed him goodnight she said, "I'm glad the mystery of the missing crisps is solved. You must be too! Still love you! Will always love you!"

Children need to know that we want them to be free to tell the truth. We reassure them that our conversations will be wrapped in insight and help, rather than criticising and humiliation. We want to encourage them to see us as the people they can always share the hard things with. By starting to refine this precious space early, and it will take multiple occasions, we free them of having to lie to avoid feelings of shame and facing unpleasant truths. By doing so we future proof them because the time will come when something serious happens and they need your help immediately, even though they may have made an awful mistake.

"MIS"BEHAVIOUR: The shame of abandonment, in respect to adoptees, foster children, and those from complex circumstances

The abandonment of a child happens for many reasons. It can occur through the bereavement of a mother or father or both. More typically it happens when a parent or parents face intolerable social stigmatisation, harm, dire financial difficulties, threats, physical and mental health issues, and drug and alcohol addictions, making it impossible to raise their child.

No parent sets out to abandon their child, but terrible situations force this awfully complicated outcome. As you likely know, Sharon and I have two adopted children, Kim and Noni. They are incredibly fine and generous women today, but it has taken them a long, long time to work through losing their first parents. This has been a process that has profoundly affected their emotion and behaviour, especially in the early years. We respect what our girls have had to work through and know with hindsight just how much their loss touched them.

Largely, they have found peace, but this deep loss took much longer for them to unravel than most appreciate. Also, Sharon and I hold their first parents in huge regard because we know that offering their children up for adoption was heartbreakingly the only option they had at the time. We took on what their parents could not, and we have always kept them in the forefront of our hearts and minds.

For Kim and Noni, for other adoptees, and many of the children in foster care, this same fact applies. They were wrenched, through no fault of their own, and without consent or understanding, from their mothers and/ or fathers. They were pre-wired to receive some very "magical" emotional needs from their first parents which never happened. This loss is significant; cut off from the quintessential source of nourishment from the people who created them. We now know that to thrive children must feel loved and emotionally attached to their first parents very early on. Anything other than this involves playing catch up.

When abandonment occurs, a child is far, far more likely to feel less – discarded, second-rate, unworthy, left out, or ashamed. It does not matter why a first parent left; the fact is they left. It is very difficult for a child's mindset to rationally absorb the enormity of abandonment. Understanding it is a life's work. Every abandoned child remains puzzled about the "Why?" "Why did my parents leave me?" As you might expect, children tend to blame themselves. This sets up a pattern of thinking reflecting shame – "Was I not good enough?" "Was I not worth it?" "Why me?" "Why couldn't they love me?" "If I wasn't enough to be loved by them, how could you love me?" "I can never be enough to be loved, can I?" When the one in the world who is meant to love and care for you leaves, it is difficult to believe that anyone who becomes important to you will not do the same in the future. As a result, children in this position can end up living with anxiety and fear and being constantly on-guard in case they are abandoned again. It becomes hard to trust others, it feels safer to call the shots, be oppositional, to get sulky or angry, to be the boss in a secret bid to self-protect. Such trust issues have the potency to prevent the formation of rich, deep, trusting relationships in childhood, and later in life.

The abandoned child suffers a deep trauma. It changes everything in their world at a time when their brain is in crucial stages of development. These children do not have the freedom to consciously choose behaviours. The behaviours they grab at, often interpreted as negative by others, are dictated by their past experiences, and are chosen simply to survive or win a moment. Disapprovals, castigations, and punishments will not change this. Instead, the child will feel more helpless and interpret the world as even more unpredictable and dangerous.

Our real work lies in helping them to see our unwavering love and commitment to them. And, when wayward behaviours must be addressed, we ensure we address the behaviour, and keep their spirit and our connection intact. We tell them this as we gently teach new skills. Over time we want them to know they matter to us, forever, and the world (particularly our world) is a better place for having them in it.

My hope is that this chapter has linked you to the inner emotional world of children; how carrying the many different versions of shame can trigger traumatic behaviour right through to subtle mood swings, and why. My intention has been to clear a pathway to help you nurture the emergence of a young person's spirit by separating their mistakes and poor choices, often based on a "faulty logic," from the beauty of who they are, and who they can become.

The "art" of REDIRECTING unwanted behaviours

6

This chapter introduces the front-line skills to redirect unwanted or undesirable behaviours. I deliberately use the word "art" in the heading because it captures a style that has principles, but the performance is remarkably human – sensitive, intuitive, adaptable, impromptu, even using your own quirkiness.

Redirection is a word efficient style that guides a child's behaviour from the unsuitable to the more suitable. The goal is to reduce the need to switch up to stronger, more assertive techniques explained in the following two chapters. To tune you into the art of redirection, I was at the airport and watched the gorgeous antics of an investigative toddler and her ingenious mother's responses. She said, simply, in the right moments, *"Oh, look at this!"* or *"Come and help me with…"* Her daughter was immediately redirected, took her hands away from the hand sanitiser and moved to investigate what had caught her mother's attention. Used in a more sophisticated way, redirection is a perfect intervention for much older children too.

Redirection is a simple and precise process, too easily overlooked, that can be used in a host of situations. We use words and phrases that are to the point and have a low emotional output. May I step you through the levels of redirection?

Redirection, level one

ACTIVITY

In this first instance, you would move close to your boys and say, using an easy-going voice tone, *"Hey, boys? It's not safe to wrestle in the house. Take it outside on the lawn."* It is best to match your style to mirror the tone you would use when speaking to your best friend's child. This is vastly different

DOI: 10.4324/9781003346715-6

to saying, *"Boys, boys, boys! Stop it! Stop it! Stop wrestling! How many times have I told you? It's not on and I'm sick of it."* This is barking orders at the boys and hoping that your cranky tone and angry gestures will convince them to "Stop wrestling!" Redirecting unwanted behaviours, on the other hand, expresses what is not working, and what needs to happen.

I witnessed redirection at level one when eight-year-old Cobi stepped out of the shop with his mother and sister.

He complained, "Where's mine. Why does she have one and I don't?"

His Mum matter-of-factly replied. "Don't stress cheeky Charlie. She saved up and got it with her money. I can help you do the same if you want to."

This technique only requires just a few well-chosen words, and very little emotional investment.

Redirection, level two

ACTIVITY

What if the wrestling boys do not cooperate following this level one redirection? Then, there is scope take it up a notch. You might move closer to them, place your hand on each of them, make eye contact, raise your eyebrows or widen your gaze, drop your voice into a lower tone and say, *"Boys, I'm serious. Take it outside, now."* With a smile, you might playfully pull one up and say, *"Off you go!"*

Redirection, level three

ACTIVITY

Let us imagine that the boys are still not listening. They are over excited and not picking up on what you want. You now take the redirection up to a third level. For this, you would move right next to them, fix your eyes to their eyes, put on your "matter of fact" face, and say in a strong, slow, flat voice, *"Time to listen."* Pause – wait two or three seconds and continue. *"Boys, are you listening?"* Pause again – wait another two or three seconds. Then, slowly and deliberately say, *"Take your wrestling on to the lawn now, if you don't, you'll miss your wrestling programme this week."* Your goal is to implement the redirection, not to escalate emotions. So, you do not show annoyance, as this is likely to feed reactive behaviour, then drama is never far behind. Showing disapproval in your facial expression and voice tone is enough to communicate what you want and what should happen.

As mentioned earlier, when you must redirect your child's behaviour, it will help to imagine you are speaking to your best friend's child. To illustrate this, imagine your best friend's son, Kai, has slept over. It is morning and he is to be picked up later in the afternoon. You are aware that both boys are tired, overexcited, and are feeling at a loose end. A short time later you hear giggling, thumping, bumping, and laughter from the other end of the house so you head off to investigate. As you walk into your bedroom, you see 11-year-old Kai completing a somersault on your new, expensive bed. Your son is cheering him on. You briskly walk up to Kai and look him straight in the eye. Firmly, without much emotion you use a low, slow voice and say, *"Kai, that's not on. Hop off and do the right thing otherwise I'll phone your mum to collect you right now. I want you both to head outside right now."* As you walk off you tell your son he should know better.

ACTIVITY

Redirection, level four

With fixed eye-contact and a strong, slow, low voice tone you firmly state, *"Tell me what I want you to be doing right now?"* You hold your gaze. Delivering this question in this way delivers a special space, a pause, for self-correction, and it works in just about any situation. Once they answer positively, you respond with, *"Thank you,"* or *"That's right,"* or *"Great, get on with it."*

In other situations, it is best to ask, *"Tell me what you should be doing right now? I'll give you a minute to think of the answer I need, then I'll be back."* This method gives a child, or children, a chance to think about their wisest choice rather than being put on the spot and pressured to reform.

Likewise, a sweet tool many use is to count to five with THAT look on your face! This buys some time for the kids to think about doing what you are asking. Over time, it becomes automatic and brings two benefits. Firstly, it helps you to respond calmly. Secondly, it provides a predictable structure to help children optimistically problem solve.

There is groundwork to be done

The benefit of coaching kids to understand personal boundaries and requests is a critical foundation to redirect behaviour and reach better outcomes. This starts very early on when we say:

"I don't want you climbing over my back. Sit on my lap instead!"
"I'll get you a drink as soon as I put the things on the bench away."
"Okay, let's sing the song one last time together, then I'm stopping."
"I don't want to play hide and seek. But I'm happy to sit with you while you play with your Lego."
"I'm going to the toilet now. Stay here, I'll be back in a few minutes."
"You ready? I'll give you one more push on the swing and then I'm sitting down."

Then, later as teens they are more likely to respond positively when we say:

"I can't drive you to Meg's right now. I'm happy to do it after lunch!"
"I'll cook dinner. Can you please put the things on the bench away? Sorry, there's so much!"
"Oh, I've had enough of this. I'll give you ten more minutes then I'm stopping."
"I really don't want to get out the car and meet people today. But I'm happy to drive you and sit in the car."
"I need to be by myself for a bit. I'm going to lie on my bed and have a read."
"I can give you half an hour to help you with this. I have to head off afterwards."

Through practicing personal boundaries and requests, we gradually, ever so gradually, teach children to listen, tune in and show empathy, respond cooperatively, and live agreeably. Our modelling also teaches them to express themselves in the same courteous way. Beyond using this as a means of redirecting behaviour, personal boundaries are required to nurture our own happiness and comfort as parents.

Non-verbal prompts

It is also wise to teach your children a few basic non-verbal prompts you can use with each other. These are hand signals to indicate *"Take it easy,"* *"Shhh,"* *"Yes,"* *"No,"* *"Sorry,"* *"Slow down,"* *"Stop,"* *"Listen to me,"* and *"Take some time out to regroup your emotions."* This way, you can give suggestions, reminders, and instructions without words. Remember, sometimes words can be triggers for intensifying tricky feelings because they carry emotion. Similarly, teach your children to use hand signals to show, *"I'm feeling frustrated," "Help me," "I'm overwhelmed," "Get me out of here,"* and *"Sorry."*

Finally, there is one additional technique in the "art" of redirection that I must not miss. Have you perfected THAT LOOK? The LOOK that says, *"Are you kidding me? This is not on! Not ever!"* This LOOK, combined with foreboding body language, has the power to stop a zombie in its tracks without a word. Many of the young people I work with call this their mother or father's "death stare" and it means business.

Tactical ignoring – a strategy to ignore unwanted behaviours that should not matter

You are forgiven for wondering how ignoring can be part of the "art" of distraction? In this instance, we are concerned with sensibly distracting ourselves. There are, of course, behaviours that we should never ignore, such as offensive, dangerous, and potentially risky ones. When a child or teen steps over the line of what is acceptable, safe, or functional, it must be addressed, along with teaching new skills that will better serve them in the future. Equally, there are many behaviours best not to give our attention to because they will be of little consequence in an hour, tomorrow, next week or ever. However, some of us as parents and educators have trained ourselves, quite accidentally over the years, to buy into too much of our children's and student's noise and turbulence. Our buy in highlights and strengthens the very behaviours we do not want.

A mixed message

An exasperated father says, *"That's it, Ayman, your behaviour is silly! How many times do I have to ask you to be sensible with your friends?"* Then, in front of all the guests, he demands Ayman go to his bedroom for time-out, and stay there till he calls him back. Ayman heads off to his room but reappears shortly thereafter with an impish look on his face. At eight years old his father feels Ayman is too old to push the boundaries like that. So, in front of guests, Dad explodes and scolds Ayman. Ayman looks shocked and somewhat upset. Dad eventually stops and the guests squirm uncomfortably. You see, deep inside Ayman's psyche he believes this gala show of words and emotion by Dad, especially in front of guests, has given him spectacular attention. Dad has reinforced Ayman's "faulty logic" that says he belongs and is valued by being excitable, funny, and over the top. So, Ayman will continue with these very same behaviours into the future. What else could Dad have done? Firstly, could Ayman's behaviour have been tactically ignored? Ayman was likely being "silly" because he was over excited with so many guests and friends at his house. Could a quiet word from Dad have redirected Ayman's behaviour? Might Dad have enlisted Ayman's help, which would have given him some structure, purpose, and predictability to work within?

If your senses are gently whispering that you do micromanage, over-control, and like to have the last word a little too often, then tactical ignoring will be challenging for you. Start to practice by setting a small goal to use this skill just once a day. This is a great way to develop a tactical ignoring mindset. I bet you are already thinking of a behaviour or two you could buy out of. Great escapes include heading off to the toilet and locking the door, sitting, and regroup your thinking, or running to the car to tidy the boot again, or heading off to weed or water the garden while the urge passes. Do anything to buy yourself a little reflective time.

As educators in classrooms, we learn fast to avoid power battles because once students sense we have entered their fight, we have lost. This moment never needs to be a public challenge to be won. As well, with young people who have learnt to battle, never ask them a "why" in front of the class. "Why" invites long-winded, irrelevant, and power-biased answers. These students do not know it but are totally reliant on poised, emotionally healthy adults to defuse situations for them. Instead, wise educators state, "I see you need help with..." Then, immediately sit with the student and show them the way, perhaps without eye contact, as it can sometimes heighten emotion. Once they are re-engaged, this talented teacher would get up and move away. If you don't have to, then do not give the unwanted behaviour power! There is no point in challenging an educator who is composed, logical, and focused on the lesson, and who responds with brief, close-ended comments such as:

"I want you to learn this so let's get on with the lesson."
"I'm happy to talk it through with you after the lesson. Not now."
"I like you too much to argue about this."
"This is the way it stays."
"This is the moment where you need to leave it. We can do this later."

Sometimes, in a classroom, we just need to roll with the punches. To go with the flow and refuse to buy into our controlling instincts. For example, a playful but pesky comment is made in class by a student. It did not hurt anyone and was short lived. Your instincts want to pull them up on it, but you choose not to. Timing is everything, and you display the emotional flexibility to look at them, switch on your smile, insert a glint of humour in your voice and quietly say, *"I can see where you're coming from. Save it for later."*

Remember, tactical ignoring is totally different to switching off, being fed up, and ignoring everything. The fact is, by not responding and rewarding some of our children's annoying and trivial behaviours, they will reduce and gradually disappear. That is a fact; please hold on to this and persevere.

PRAISE – an effective way to direct and redirect behaviour

Behaviour-specific praise is a positive technique that encourages children and adolescents to want to do better (for more on praise, see Chapter 9, The STAR ACT – praise and building credit). By catching the behaviours we value, and reducing our passion for "calling out" the behaviours we do not want, we greatly increase the chances of seeing more desirable behaviours within an optimistic atmosphere.

Behaviour-specific praise begins with a change in mindset. It is the best way to increase the frequency of the behaviours we want to see more of. Let me explain. Eight-year-old Anni is with friends. They are at the table drawing and are sharing the coloured pencils. Anni often becomes single minded, wanting to own the pencils, and can easily forget to share. So, as the group works together you might say, every so often, *"I love the way you're sharing the pencils together. Way to go!"* or more specifically, *"Anni? Thanks for helping Madi find the red pencil,"* or *"You are such kind kids together."*

To be most effective, behaviour-specific praise relies on us being tuned in to what is happening for our children, and which moments are likely to be more challenging. Allow me to use a strange analogy to expand on what being tuned into a child's behaviour looks like. I see the progression of so-called minor "MIS"behaviour to more serious "MIS"behaviour as a series of chunky links that form a heavy chain stretched across a gateway. In the beginning, the behaviour may be a little thoughtless, silly, or your child might have the zoomies! At this point the first link in the chain glows, ever so faintly. The glow is barely visible to the unaware, untrained, or distracted eye. Then, as the behaviour intensifies, the links at the midway point of the chain begin to glow a soft red. Now the glow is noticeable. Then, with almost exponential speed, our child's emotion and behaviour rocket to the last several links on the other side of the chain where they are glowing white hot! What do we learn from this simple analogy? The art of redirection is far more successful when applied earlier rather than later. When emotion and behaviour amp up, it is much harder for children with hot brains to stop, listen, and cooperate. Early intervention is always easier and best!

Playing it forward

14-year-old Arlo's experience provides an example of how to use praise, very specifically, to direct behaviour in the direction we want it to go. Arlo is bright, and somewhat of a sporting legend, but has always been quick to criticise his 12-year-old sister for almost anything, most of the time.

Prior to her returning home, his mother, Bek, finds the right moment to say, *"Arlo? Beth received best and fairest for her basketball this morning. She's feeling really pleased and I want you to congratulate her, so she knows you're pleased for her. You know she looks up to you."*

Later, when everyone is together, Arlo delivers a simple compliment to Beth, *"Good job, Beth!"* under Bek's watchful gaze. She acknowledges and reinforces his effort with a wink. Being positive and proactive produces better outcomes than directing energy into catch up or trying to repair damage following an unfortunate event.

7 | The "art" of HOLDING A CHILD ACCOUNTABLE, with poise

Holding a child accountable for their actions, using kindness and strength, in a moment when they have been thoughtless or unravelled takes a special awareness and courage. It is the essence of the style we explored in the Authoritative quadrant (Chapter 2, Which QUADRANT reflects your PARENTING or TEACHING style?). This style of interaction resists the traditional retaliatory responses where a parent or educator surrenders their kindness in the heat of the moment, and irritably barks threats or punishments at a child. Those who are prone to using this style mistakenly convince themselves that punishment, somehow, offers a solution. It does not have any such capacity.

First, get your emotions in the right place

In the instant when we must deal with a child's or student's "MIS"behaviour we can easily become victims of our own heightened emotions. An unbridled flush of emotion is no help because our children's composure relies, wholly, on ours. While none of us will ever achieve perfect emotional regulation, there is abundant scope to get this instant right because how we handle our own emotions sends two compelling messages to young people. The first is in what we model. How we respond in awkward, difficult, or chaotic moments teaches our children to use the very same behaviours in moments they find awkward, difficult, or heated. Secondly, what we say and do right now will have a powerful impact on what happens next. When we give in to our runaway emotions we are likely to overreact

DOI: 10.4324/9781003346715-7

and overwhelm our kids. This high-level emotional input stirs feelings of disconnection, shame, and defeat which can often leave them resentful, brooding, and distrusting.

As much as we can, it is best to remain poised, gently reach out, and draw them closer to us. This reinforces our connection and a desire to fix it together. As a parent, we may even kiss them on the head and say, *"It's okay. We'll talk later. What can we do to help fix this?"* You may well discuss your child's mistake or carelessness later, but in the meantime, this clever, connecting intervention has buoyed this child's composure, kept their dignity, and left them in a malleable position where they are open to guidance, shortly. Helping them to stay emotionally attached allows a precious space where they might naturally feel a little regret and want to make changes, rather than being forced to.

A LEARNING OPPORTUNITY: Parents reflect on the past

I recall asking the parents of triplets (their boys are now in their mid-20s), whether they would manage them any differently if they had their time over again. This brilliantly open couple both laughed and needed no time to think. There were two things they instantly shared!

Firstly, Christie admitted to feeling embarrassed because it took her at least the first 12 years of parenting to learn she was not the better parent. She reached across and held Sunny's hand tightly to reassure him that this was her shortcoming and had been inspired by her own apprehensions. Christie added that hindsight had also revealed that Sunny had been a wonderfully connected father to the boys, but she found it hard to give him the grace to parent using his own style in the early years.

Secondly, both wished they had removed the emotional heat and urgency they often brought into the tricky moments with their sons. Once again, hindsight offered them the space to see their emotionally driven responses never helped an already volatile situation. They now understood the opposite intervention would have been so much more productive. But as young, well-motivated parents who desperately loved their boys, they believed that every "MIS"behaviour had to be stomped on. At the time they were blind to seeing the wonderful values they had already passed on to their precious boys.

The first response to a child's "MIS"behaviour is NOT to fix the "MIS"behaviour

There is a reason for every child's behaviour. Their behaviour is an attempt to express a need, whether they are four, fourteen, or older, whether they are your child, or a student in your classroom. "MIS"behaviour alerts us to stop, take notice, and really think about what is likely driving it. Sitting under every behaviour is an emotional driver and we must scratch below the annoyance of "MIS"behaviour and work out what need is driving it.

When our efforts only aim to stomp out behaviours we do not want, we place ourselves in a position to become emotionally triggered. We form a negative pattern of action where we tend to match a child's elevated emotions and difficult behaviour with our own elevated emotions and difficult behaviour. With the understandings we have today, this can never be justified. As mentioned previously, the result is we are rewarding and strengthening the very behaviours in our children we do not like or want – "Monkey see, monkey do!" Or worse, we are ignoring some very real problems being faced by our child. Children continue behaviour when they feel it is being rewarded and there is nothing like the screeching of a parent that rewards so richly.

Despite the inconvenience of "MIS"behaviour, in more than 90% of cases it is perfectly normal for young human beings. It is a sign of normalcy for children and teens to push the limits so that they can work out how far those limits go. Many children once labelled as immature, silly, naughty, challenging, even oppositional, later become fine adults. If you do not share this more common background, then it is likely you will be sorely tested by a child who acts out their emotions. So, can we agree? The goal to holding children accountable, with poise, is to build their empathy and personal responsibility, not to achieve a short-lived obedience. This goal can be easily missed because this is a messy work in progress that ebbs and flows.

What follows are the steps to hold children accountable, with grace, love, and skilful leadership. By developing this technique our emotional steadiness will improve too. As it does, our children and students will feel closer to us. They will be better able to reflect on their actions and make amends. They are less likely to repeat the "MIS"behaviour in the future.

PRACTICAL STEPS: Holding children accountable (with poise)

1. **Decide on the behaviours you will hold children accountable for**
   The behaviours you choose should reflect your strongest family or classroom ideals and values: kindness, respect, helpfulness, safety, and personal hygiene. You might frame these simply and positively:

   - We try to be kind to each other.
   - We listen thoughtfully to each other.
   - We help one another.
   - We try our best.
   - We use words that show we care.
   - We show compassion and help others who need support.

2. **Choose your battles wisely**
   Allow 90% of children's awkward or irritating behaviours to slip by. Pick up on the 10% that really do matter. Hindsight tells us that so many annoying and stubborn behaviours drop out with maturity. Yet, a few adults who have the same rigid and reactive traits as their child fail to see this. These poor souls will not shift their pattern of "tight control" and "having the last say" wreaks serious relational damage.

3. **Stop and move**
   When an issue arises, and it falls into the 10% of behaviours you must address, stop what you are doing. Instead of raising your voice and calling through the house, or from the other side of the classroom, go to the child or to the group.

4. **As you move towards them check your emotions**
   If you are feeling emotional allow the flush to pass. As mentioned earlier, when a child is struggling with their behaviour, an emotionally discombobulated adult is not helpful. Even if you must fake it at first, you need to look composed, strong, and kind. They will draw strength from your composure. A good way to keep your emotions in check is to use this personal three-point scale. It is a logical approach because it allows you quantify and measure your feelings.

Your Personal three-point scale

ACTIVITY

LEVEL THREE (your highest level of pressure)

Admit to yourself that you are totally annoyed. And, you have every right to feel this way. Also recognise that your child, or this student, cannot regulate their behaviour or emotions in this moment. This must be your moment to shine, just for two or three minutes, and to do this you must be in control of your own emotions. Engage all your resources so that you do not enter their fight. This is not about winning or getting them to instantly reform or obey. They may comply, but the focus is on modelling the healthiest communication style possible in this tricky moment. Teach by example – they will watch and learn from this, and from all you do!

LEVEL TWO (mid-range of pressure)

Acknowledge that you are feeling irritated. Breathe. Take another deep breath and check your own emotional state. Are you tired and fatigued? Or are your emotional reserves topped up aplenty? If you must buy some time, tell your child, or student, you are on the way. At home you can buy time by going to the toilet first or pretend to get something from the car. It is more difficult in a classroom but one idea may be to pretend to help a likeable student on the way so you take a moment to channel your best self. Shake off any heightened emotion. Your goal is to be composed and to lead, so keep on breathing. Prepare yourself.

LEVEL ONE (lowest level of pressure)

Acknowledge that you are feeling mildly annoyed and that is okay! Ask yourself:

"Is this behaviour worth buying into?"
"What's likely driving it?"
"Will it matter in an hour?"
"Will I even remember it in 24 hours?"
"Is it worth tactically ignoring?"
"Is there an easy circuit breaker, or redirection, that could be applied?"
"What's the simplest way to redirect their behaviour?"

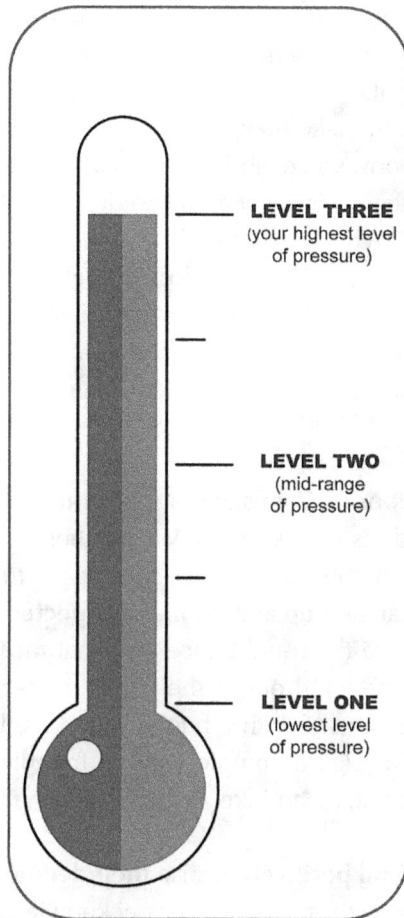

LEVEL THREE
(your highest level
of pressure)

LEVEL TWO
(mid-range
of pressure)

LEVEL ONE
(lowest level
of pressure)

Figure 7.1 Your personal three-point scale including levels one, two and three

5. **Be with them, bring yourself to their height, and connect**

   Use their name and a warm voice. Some eye contact is important, but do not overdo it. Too much can provoke embarrassment or shame which then triggers an immediate defensive reaction and in turn triggers even trickier behaviours. When there is a greater sense of urgency, elevate your voice, and if it is your own child, touch them and stay composed.

6. **Explain the difficulty in less than ten words**

   Do not justify, defend, or get too wordy. You know my mantra. In moments like this... *"Fewer words are more powerful."* For younger children, tell them what is going on and what is best to do. For older kids, state what the problem is, and that you want them to make their best choice to fix it.

7. **Encourage them to make their best choice**

   Use your face, body, voice, and hand gestures to reinforce your vote of confidence in them. This is not a time to demand, threaten, or tell them to "Calm down." When any individual is told to "Calm down," backed into a corner, or suffers a sudden loss of dignity, they will say and do things that are out of character. You can, if appropriate, coolly state that you will follow through with a consequence if they choose not to make a wise choice. But do it matter-of-factly with a low emotional investment.

8. **Walk away**

   Walking away stops us from standing over our kids and appearing too demanding. And, as you walk away offer them a vote of confidence. Smile, pop your thumbs up and say, *"You've got this!"*

9. **Occasionally change it up and do the unexpected**

   Sometimes, change the usual dance step that most of us get stuck in. You might take the wind out of their sails by using humour. Many a situation can be diffused with a hug, a wink, a silly face, a poked-out tongue, a dare, a joke, a zombie walk, a friendly eye roll, a thumbs up, a kind comment, a dad joke, or by simply changing the subject. Be strategic.

10. **When they respond positively, praise their decision making**

    There is no need to throw a party, just acknowledge their great choice and move on.

11. **The "art" to follow-up, or private conversations**

    Sometimes you will model strength, kindness, and display wonderful skills in a tricky moment, but your child does not respond in the way you had hoped. You do enough to get through the challenging situation, however you decide you must move to a higher level of accountability. In this instance, you opt for a follow-up or private conversation. See follow-up or private conversations as coaching, not a time for tell-offs or disapprovals. Meet privately away from siblings or other students, review what happened and explain what they need to do next time (build the skills). Do this within the context that they are valued and this is a natural work in progress. When this balance is struck a child or teen is more likely to be on board.

I use the expression... *"Never strike when the iron is hot! Always when it's cold."* In other words, let the dust settle. Generally, you would have a private conversation later once everyone is breathing more easily. When the time is right, talk about what happened. Show your warmth. Be your kindest, most poised self. As well, this is the moment to use your instinct because there are two options to choose from here:

Option one

Ask:

> *"Are you okay?"*
> *"Hey? You're such a great kid (or student). Tell me what happened earlier on?"*
> *"I know you're disappointed. What happened?"*
> *"Don't be too tough on yourself. We can fix this."*
> *"I can see you're not happy. How can we make this better?"*
> *"All of us make mistakes."*
> *"We all learn from our mistakes. They're our best teacher."*
> *"It looks like you're having a hard time. Let me help?"*
> *"Can you explain what happened?"*
> *"Would you like to talk about it?"*

Listen, try to appreciate their position, and consider it. Validate their feelings; *"Oh? I can see why you feel that..."* or *"I understand, you know we can..."* This is likely to spark a healthy discussion and they may have a perspective that you missed.

In the right moment, insert how they could have expressed their feelings or handled the situation more constructively. It is acceptable to say you were disappointed in their behaviour or choice, but guard against saying you are disappointed in them as this arouses hurt. State what you expect them to do next time. An alternative, with your child, is to bundle them into the car with you. The car offers privacy, safety from too much eye-contact, and its movement provides a mild, comfortable distraction. Never underestimate the value of this forum!

Option two

This option is ideal for children and adolescents who react badly to direct questions such as, *"Why did you do that?"* or *"What were you thinking?"* Their answer is likely to be, *"Dunno"* or *"Whatever"* with a shoulder shrug.

87

Make a promise to yourself – never ask such questions when you know your child or a particular student will answer in this way because it simply provokes their anger.

Also, some children are not able to articulate what happened because they are still processing their feelings. Others will know "why," but answering it incites feelings of antagonism, perhaps shame. This does not mean you have a child with oppositional defiant disorder. Far from it. What it suggests is that you have a child who uses anger and opposition to deflect their perceived loss of dignity. Be smart and emotionally sensitive. Try to understand how they think.

You might begin the private conversation with, *"I'm sorry about earlier on,"* or *"I'm sorry that didn't work out,"* or *"I feel badly,"* or *"I agree. This is upsetting…"* or *"I want to help. What can I do?"* Such empathic statements provide a beautifully disarming start to a private conversation. If a conversation ensues, gently ask a question or two as this will help them process their feelings and thoughts. If your child or student does not want to talk, respect this, and briefly state what you expect them to do next time. Finally, summarise the situation, give it hope, and find a way to show confidence in them.

During private conversations choose your words carefully and use connecting facial and body language. At home, lying on a bed or on the floor together, is a nice way to minimise eye contact and focus on words. At school, if you are sitting, try not to have furniture between you and the student. It becomes a blocker to words and feelings. Rather than sitting face to face, sit side by side turning in towards each other as it is less confronting.

When you need to challenge, be sure you also convey one of the strengths you most admire about them. Warmly ask questions but avoid interrogating. Children and young adolescents rarely cooperate with adults who take the high moral ground, subject them to the third degree, or take away the necessary wiggle room to keep dignity.

Always give you child or student a candid picture, packaged in kindness, about what went wrong and what is best to do next time. If they do not know, they cannot change it. If you will not tell them, then someone else with less compassion and care for them will. Finally, young people of all ages do so much better with parents and teachers who are real, who during private conversations gently prepare them to expect and cope with the inevitable rough spells life will throw at them. Unfair, hurtful, and unpredictable situations will occur – we deal with them without drama, we learn, they pass, and mostly we grow.

The "art" of APPLYING AN EDUCATIVE CONSEQUENCE, and staying emotionally connected

8

Positive consequences nurture and strengthen the behaviours we value. These come through our encouragement and praise. Positive consequences also include having fun, laughing, chatting, and playing with our children, being with them when they play sport, doing something unexpected and enjoyable, even using a token economy system where tangible rewards may be involved.

Educative consequences, on the other hand, are planned responses that occur following a child's "MIS"judgment or "MIS"behaviour. More exactly, you initiate them when your child or student ignores your help, advice, direction, or guidance and continues to do the very thing you asked them not to.

So, what should educative consequence look like?

Do we take things away?
If so, what kinds of things?
Do we deny freedoms, rights, privileges, and events they are looking forward to?
When do we apply this style of consequence?
How long should a consequence last?
Should we fake "professional anger" to make a point?
Does the consequence need to be severe so it will be long remembered?
How should we do this?

DOI: 10.4324/9781003346715-8

The guiding principles of EDUCATIVE CONSEQUENCES

- When possible, link the consequence to the tricky or challenging behaviour that occurred.
- Be respectful by remaining emotionally connected.
- The consequence must be affectionately applied. There is no room for superiority, the flaunting of power, nastiness, or spite.
- It must be fair and considerate. Never overblow it. Less is better.
- As much as you can, make the consequence beneficial. In other words, it contains an idea that is constructive, helpful, or assists to build a skill.

EDUCATIVE CONSEQUENCES can be broken down into three broad types

1. **If you break it or mess up, then you fix it**

   In this category we guide young people to fix, as best they can, any problem they have caused. But we do not do this hastily or clumsily. We remain poised and considered. For example, your daughter makes an awfully unkind remark to another child and hurts their feelings. Later, you counsel her without invoking humiliation, and then support her to offer a sincere apology, in some way, to help repair the damage she caused. This helps her to appreciate differences and remain respectful and tolerant.

Another example may be that your son kicks a hole in the plasterboard wall during an angry outburst. If they have the financial resources, they could contribute to the repair. Better still, when you are both in a happier space, you head off to the hardware store, buy a repair kit and you work together on the repair. Try to enjoy the time you spend with them! I know a mother who did this nine times with her son over 16 months. She showed the patience of a saint and was finally rewarded when in the middle of the last repair her son said, *"I need to stop doing this Mum. There's better things I should be doing on a Saturday afternoon."* That was it. He stopped.

2. Loss of privilege

Be mindful to link the educative consequence as a natural consequence to the "MIS"behaviour that occurred. There is a universal link that many clever parents use. Allow me to share! It is bringing their child's bed-time on that day forward by 20, or 30, or 45 minutes. I recall a dad role-playing how he does this with his son to establish my response. He dropped to his knees, so he was the same height as me sitting in my seat. He reached out gently with both hands and held one of my arms and kindly said, *"I'm so sorry you lost your temper and made things so hard for yourself and your Mum. That's not like you and I know you feel bad. You know the little tricks you could have used when you started to feel frustrated, but you chose not to use them. This tells me you're tired, so I'll help you get to bed a little earlier for some great sleep. You think of a story Mum or I can read with you later, at bedtime."* And all of this is still with the usual story, hugs, and loves!

When it is too tricky to link the behaviour to a natural consequence, a sensible fall-back position is to link the "MIS"behaviour to the child making a small but meaningful positive contribution. At home extra contributions may include washing, vacuuming the car, sweeping, mopping, packing, window cleaning, or unpacking the dishwasher, taking out the rubbish or recyclables, raking leaves, cleaning windows, pulling weeds, and so on. And quite seriously, one of the best ways for this to unfold is for you to cheerfully participate with them. This is a world away from the punishing and isolating techniques many educators and parents endured as children.

Classic examples of "loss of privilege" may include taking away a video game, phone, iPad, or access to television for a short time, or missing out on something coming up such as no longer being able to attend a party, go to sports practice, play an upcoming match, or go out with friends.

For younger children who are not playing considerately with others, even though we have shown them what to do, we simply remove them. Later, after a little coaching, we bring them back, and find a way for them to be successful. We praise them as soon as they are! Alternatively, we can remove the play from the child. This means we remove the toy, or whatever they are playing with, if they ignore our request and help to redirect. Later, we bring the toy back, and engineer a way for them to be successful. We always follow up with praise when they do it better.

3. The gift of time – "time-in" or "time-out"? How?

The gift of time refers to how we go about supporting our children to stay in-charge of their feelings or regain control of them. Now we are beginning to talk about emotional self-regulation. This is the ability to manage one's feelings effectively, not perfectly, when under pressure. From a developmental perspective, self-regulation takes much, much longer to develop than most of us would like to think. It takes more than the first 20 years of our lives for that vital wiring up in the brain to be completed. In addition, we know that children with self-regulatory difficulties are usually wrestling with emotional immaturities, traumatic histories, and a range of disabilities. This, of course, slows the wiring up and can compromise it.

This leads us to consider the differences between "time-out" and "time-in." I think the time-out method is better than the harsher traditional punishing approaches, but when executed aggressively, "time-out" has the same damaging potentials. Personally, I do not support a parent regularly shouting, *"Get to your bedroom for time-out"* to their child. Nor do I support a teacher yelling, *"Get out of my classroom and get to the office!"* I have seen it really ramp up emotionality in children because it delivers the idea that the bedroom or the office are prisons. Then, the prison break is never far behind!

At home, however, bedrooms can become fabulous places to retreat to, to regroup emotions. Just as you likely have a book by your bed that has the power to transport your mind somewhere else, be sure your children have access to mindfulness approaches and activities that offer them this very same advantage. Another popular place kids enjoy retreating to is that squishy space between the back of the couch and the wall with cushions to lay on! It is all about giving them structure, space, time, and dignity to regroup their emotions!

So, the next time your child is emotionally dysregulated you might say, *"Spend a few moments in your bedroom with your glitter jars (or...). They always help you feel better!"* In tough moments, when they cannot find the words they need, teach them to use a simple "time-out" signal. This universal signal alerts you to their frazzled feeling and the need for help. No one needs to talk. Just being supported while frazzled feelings pass is the goal.

We are at the beginning of this new emotional journey in schools, and it's gathering momentum globally. Many schools are creating classrooms and purpose-built rooms filled with self-regulating and interoception equipment. Progressive leaderships are training all staff and students how to use these resources, and this approach and these spaces are proving to be transformative. They actively teach students how to self-manage their emotions on an everyday basis. What an investment to maximise great mental health in children and youth.

This is the perfect segue to Dan Siegel's hand model of the brain (Siegel, 2012). It's a visual representation of what happens in people's brains when too many strong feelings happen all at once. In such moments, Dan says our brain "flips its lid" and his brain-hand model helps us understand. Teach your children and students this.

First, hold up your fist with your thumb tucked into the centre of it. Turn your fist to the side so your kids are looking at a profile of the brain. Get them to do the same. The fingers wrapped around your thumb represent the brain's prefrontal cortex. The brain's prefrontal cortex does all our clever thinking and helps us solve problems.

The thumb represents the limbic area connected to the prefrontal cortex, and to the brainstem. The limbic area takes in information from the body and helps to regulate breathing, digestion, and heart function. It also has the amygdala, which creates the fight, flight, freeze, and faint response that happens when we feel threatened.

When brain systems are not connected the brain becomes unbalanced like a wobbly washing machine – it's chaotic, wild, and rigid. Now, flip your fingers and thumb right out and explain to your children this is what happens when we "lose it" or when we "flip our lids." Look at your fingers; the prefrontal cortex is no longer connected and cannot work. And look at your thumb (our feelings). Our feelings are no longer being kept safe by our prefrontal cortex, but are hanging out, unprotected, and hurting by a compromised limbic system.

What you have just done is powerful. This is a magical way to teach how emotion can dysregulate the brain. The amygdala might be useful when it comes to fighting or running away, but it's useless when solving complex people problems that involve emotions. Having this knowledge is a big help to improve our response to emotional situations. As well, we know from brain imaging studies that this information helps direct our attention to areas that help activate the regions capable of supporting us. This is a fact.

Here are a few mindfulness activities that my clients use to prevent them from "flipping their lid" or to help them recover:

- Put in earpieces and listen to your play list.
- Box breathing – see www.youtube.com/watch?v=n6RbW2LtdFs
- Pinwheel breathing – see www.youtube.com/watch?v=HYZ2PTyJkzg
- Bunny breathing – see www.youtube.com/watch?v=XYGEvi0VJpY
- Christopher Willard, in his book, *ALPHABREATHS: The ABC's of Mindful Breathing for Kids*, uses play, imagination, and breathing to help children regroup their emotions. He suggests:

  - Dolphin breath. Breathe in as you lift your arms up high. Breathe out as you imagine diving into the ocean. Repeat several times or more.
  - Elevator breath. As you breathe in, imagine your breath going all the way up to the top floor of your belly. As you breathe out, imagine it going all the way down to the bottom. You can even count floors as you breathe. Repeat several times or more.
  - Teddy bear breath. Lie down on your back and put a teddy bear on your tummy. As you breathe in and out, watch your teddy bear go up and down. Repeat several times or more.

- Paint or colour by number or code or do a "dot to dot."
- Go do your hobby – Lego, tomboy, knitting, or crochet!
- Take a long walk or run.
- Play with a fidget toy.
- Listen to a meditation.
- Colour in a mandala.
- Redesign your mini-Zen garden.
- Bounce on a mini trampoline.
- Wrap them up in a big tight sheet or get them under a weighted blanket.
- View your kaleidoscope or goo timer collection.
- Explore and use the apps "Buddhify" and "Smiling Mind."

Best results occur when children are encouraged to practice one or two of these ideas often, and in the good times, to embed them. Getting into a habit reinforces the new pattern of behaviour, and soon the new option becomes an automatic choice in the tougher times.

Time-in

Time-in is a thoroughly positive parenting tool that can easily be adapted for classroom use. It occurs when you and your child spend five minutes or so on the couch, a bed, or on the floor following a difficulty or an upset. It provides a chance for them to move away from the problem, to feel connected with you, share what happened, decide what to do next and take a few minutes to regroup emotions (Doucleff and Greenhalgh, 2019). You might both listen to music or read independently as emotions calm. **Or**, when your child is being disruptive or upsetting to others, and will not listen to your redirection, simply get them to sit with you. This time together can be silent, instructive, reflective, and healing.

Many clever educators teach their children how to do a simple body scan (for example, see www.youtube.com/watch?v=xLoK5rOl8Qk) while lying together. They coach them to close their eyes and start the scan at the top of their body – the head. First, we ask them to think about their head and neck. Does it feel relaxed, tense, tired, or okay? Then they ask these same questions as they move gradually to their shoulders, arms, hands, chest, back, legs, and feet. If they find a problem while doing the scan, they breathe it out with three slow, deep breaths. We teach them not to fix anything. Their job is to find the problem and let their brain and body work together through the breathing.

I must stress that while a legitimate place exists for educative consequences, they must be applied far less frequently than praise. They are used to convey a plain message. It is, *"I'm sorry, your behaviour went too far, but more to the point, you chose not to listen to my advice, not to respond to my request and refused to adapt or help."* When praise and educative consequences are cleverly applied together, they will change a child's behaviour, positively.

Occasionally, when I raise the "art" of applying an educative consequence, a few parents say, *"Oh, you don't understand. The option of giving any sort of negative styled consequence to my child adds to his anxiety which destroys him and me!"* I do understand. More than you know. This chapter is concerned with the "art" of educative consequence because sometimes, we must draw a line in the sand, and doing this with composure, self-confidence and connection is truly an "art" to be learned.

I remember a parent who wrote, *"I've never taken anything from my children, or said they can't attend a play date or party due to bad behaviour. I don't do punishments. Never have and never will. It's cruel and traumatising."* I respect a parent's freedom and rights to raise their children in the way they see fit. However, this chapter has nothing to do with punishment. I reject punishment because it is grounded in negative emotions such as annoyance, anger, fear, frustration, and retribution. **Punishment is not linked to a child's behaviour; it is all about our unmanageable reaction in a difficult moment. As mentioned previously, it does not solve a problem. Nor does it cherish the sanctity of emotional connection.**

A personal insight – my lightbulb moment

I got angry with our eldest over something she'd done at school that reflected badly on her and on us as a family. She was just nine years old and with hindsight, had misread a situation. Again, with hindsight, I know she found it difficult to pick up on social cues, so struggled to respond appropriately at times. I was feeling mortified by what she'd done. To make things worse, we lived in a small rural community where gossip spread like wildfire, and this only added to my humiliation.

So, I confronted her. No, I didn't confront her. Let me be honest. I attacked her with awfully damaging words. I walked away and immediately felt conflicted and awfully regretful.

As I contemplated my reaction an image from the distant future crept into my mind. It was an image of my children at my funeral, and it stirred me to think. What do I want them to be saying about me on this day? What are the memories that I want to leave them with? Do I want them to remember me as a loving and emotionally safe parent, even in the trickiest of moments? Do I want their memories coloured by my kindness and care, or consumed by my overblown responses?

I have no idea why my thinking headed into this direction, but I'm grateful it did. In that moment it dawned on me that the building of these memories in my precious girls is completely my responsibility. My fight wasn't with her. It was a personal struggle within me. When we take our children's "MIS"behaviour personally the chance of calling on punishment is only ever a heartbeat away.

Punishment says, *"You must think like me and do exactly what I say, and if you don't, you will suffer until you make the choice I want."* Punishment does not respect a child's right to decide, even if their decision is a poor one. Children need the scope to make poor decisions, mistakes, and flawed judgements as these can be wonderful teachers. So, relish the moment when your child makes an impulsive or poor choice, and engineer what follows to become a considerate learning experience.

FINAL THOUGHTS: On the "art" of applying EDUCATIVE CONSEQUENCES

Frame it

We must present a clear picture to our kids about what will happen when they respond optimistically as well as what will happen when they respond unhelpfully. This means that following a difficult moment, when your child has ignored your instructions, requests, reminders, or help, they understand that you will apply an educative consequence and what this is likely to be. This knowledge does away with us overreacting in the heat of the moment, shouting out threats, and worsening an already tense situation.

Mix it up!

I remember meeting a parent at a workshop. Others were in earshot, so he leaned in close to me, lowered his voice, and said, *"Mark we've taken everything away from our son, there's nothing left in his bedroom."*

This moment has always stuck with me, and it is a reminder that a narrow, one-dimensional punitive approach never works. Indeed, it can incite hostility and rebellion in young people. Quite swiftly, children learn the art of power-based management techniques and begin to mimic their parents. If you must take things away sometimes, take them away for a short time, simply to make an instructive point. A preoccupation on banning, taking items away, and removing privileges for days on end is dangerous. Just as dangerous is when a parent shouts, *"Well, because you didn't listen, I'm not getting what I was thinking of getting you."* This is not a consequence. This is a frustrated parent flaunting their supposed power!

Timing is everything

Consequences should be calmly announced and humanely applied immediately after the behavioural "MIS"fire for our younger children. This way, a child clearly understands what they did. For children under five years, you might say, *"Because you hit your brother with your doll, I am taking your doll away for the rest of the afternoon. You can have it back after dinner and I want you to be kinder to your brother and your doll!"* You remove the doll and place it out of sight.

For older children, we announce that their "MIS"fire has attracted a consequence soon after the event, but we do not have to immediately state what the consequence will be. It is not wise to deliver a consequence when a child's emotional state, or ours, is already stretched to the limit. It is better to deliver the consequence later in the day when you are both feeling calmer. When you do this, offer the consequence matter-of-factly. Avoid over-explaining or justifying it. Most importantly, deliver it with kindness, composure, and fairness. Another emotional outburst may be triggered. Your child might explode, saying:

> *"You don't know me."*
> *"I don't care about your stupid consequences!"*
> *"Nothing you can do will change it."*
> *"You're not the boss of me!"*

I know it is hard but do not enter the fray and bite back. When we bite back and enter the fight, we relinquish leadership. Strategically, do your best to not buy into your child's heated emotions, especially when directed squarely at you. Stay poised, and simply follow through with the one consequence that you had previously chosen.

It is YOUR choice

Children do not choose the consequence, the adult does. Once it has been announced, always follow through. A consequence cannot be renegotiated or worked off by a child. Otherwise, they learn not to listen in the first place, because our boundaries are rubbery, and they can always bargain their way out of being held accountable. Once the consequence has been chosen, there is no point in challenging an adult who remains composed and does not rely on having the last say with a sting in their tail. Our children are hugely reliant on our poise! Parents and educators who do best develop closed statements such as these:

"I can see you're upset. But what's done is done."
"I love you too much to argue about this."
"It is what it is."
"I know it feels tough, but it's the way it stays."
"This is how it is going to be."
"That's it. It's done."
"We're both worked up. Let's leave it and pick up later."

Staying emotionally connected

Staying emotionally connected with your child, especially after you have delivered an educative consequence that will occur later, is crucial. As a parent, you would still go and get an ice-cream, or go to the movies, or shoot goals together if it were promised earlier. This is in stark contrast to a few who think that withdrawing affection by being huffy, sulky, and emotionally detached from kids is a vital part of the consequence. It is never acceptable, for a parent or educator, to go into sulky mode and withdraw connection from children to make a point about how seriously they should take the consequence. Nor is it acceptable to pretend to be angry to make a point. Today we understand that when an adult deliberately feigns anger or switches off emotionally from a child, it is on the spectrum of "emotional manipulation" and/or "child abuse." Not only is it damaging, but our emotional withdrawal will instinctively ramp up negative behaviours within children as they awkwardly work to reconnect.

That space where children can thrive

The best educative consequence is to build a space where children are gently encouraged to reflect on their part, and feel a need to repair the damage, upset, or harm they have caused. Teaching children from the earliest of ages how to sincerely make amends is an invaluable life skill and allows a more empathic young human to grow but it is slow, painstaking work. So, instead of responding harshly, reach out, put your arm around them, pull them closer to you and ask...

"Are you okay?"
"I can see you're upset. What happened?"
"Is there anything I can do to help?"
"Don't be too tough on yourself. You can fix it?"
"How can you make this better? I'm happy to help?"

Our mission must be to get better and better at deliberately building a space that inspires children and teens alike to step up, make amends and repair. Teach them the skills to use a soft voice, to show sorrow and be kind in the face of tension and uncertainty. Ensure they learn the very thing we do in our lives after we mess up! By starting on it early, there is plenty of time for practice, to help these skills to grow. As it blossoms, children will thrive, and will learn to take care of their mistakes and poor choices.

Sometimes, the oddest of consequences can be beautifully disarming and effective.

The case of a woolly jumper

I work with two boys, Ron and Jack, aged eight and nine years. They are fast and competitive, and their mum has a wonderful sense of humour. When her boys are cross with each other, will not give in, and refuse to find a win/win solution she slides a huge woolly jumper over both. They are trapped in the jumper together, and face to face! The habit she has built for them is that they look at each other, burst into laughter, drop to the floor, forgive, get out of the jumper, and move on.

This may not work for you, and I am not recommending it. But please recognise the bigger picture here. What this thoughtful mother is doing, so uniquely, is teaching her boys compromise, forgiveness, and how to move on. It is brilliant! She will not accept that it is okay for her boys to fight, bite, and run, or fight, bite, and hold a grudge. She is teaching them how to own what they have done, to repair the damage caused and re-establish the relationship, with a little humour. This clever mum is assisting them to learn the very skills we do in our own lives after we have a cross word or mess up.

9

The STAR ACT
Praise and building credit

Want to see more of the behaviours you value from your children or students, no matter their age?

Want to support kids to build a new behaviour?

Want to help a child substitute a concerning behaviour with a more functional one?

When trying to increase the frequency of desirable behaviours, our starting point is praise. Praise is the star act. What follows in this chapter is not rocket science, but it needs to be understood on a deeply human level, then applied consistently. Yes, I acknowledge that consistency can be an elusive commodity in the commotion of everyday life. Just do the best you can!

Praise is priceless. It shows both younger and older children that we are paying attention, have an interest in what they are doing and that we feel pride in their efforts. To be effective praise must be delivered in the right way. A great beginning is to deliver it in the same way you would convey it to an intelligent friend. Keep it short and genuine with a focus on the process (what they did). Also, it must be pitched modestly – without fanfare, hype, or using an excited, high-pitched baby-styled voice. In addition, some children do not respond well to praise given in front of others. For these beautifully sensitive souls keep your praise short and sweet and do it privately.

You might say:

"You did a great job cleaning your room. Thanks."
"I was so proud of your performance. All that rehearsing paid off."
"You made a good decision."
"You did that even though it wasn't easy."

DOI: 10.4324/9781003346715-9

"Great job!"
"Fabulous effort."
"That really helped. Thanks."
"Good for you, you didn't give up."
"I can see that you're becoming more…"
"I saw how hard you tried at…"

We have learnt that when children are praised for their hard work, or the process they have been engaged in, they begin to see they have personal power over their life and outcomes. We refrain from saying "good girl" or "good boy" as this is best for our puppies at puppy school. We have also discovered praise directed at a personal level sees the person receiving the praise wanting to pull back on future efforts. As strange as it seems, this is a protective mechanism to minimise what psychology calls "risk to self."

And here is the word on fake praise, or a style of praise that is over-inflated. It is very unwise and can be harmful. Studies show younger people with low self-esteem actually shrank from new challenges when adults use a gushy, highly motivated style that was exaggerated and overblown (Brummelman et al., 2014). Here is a perfect example of this overstated style for 11-year-old Antonio:

"Oh, Antonio, you're fabulous! Good boy! You've made my day, mate, because you got your shoes on. Now let me do the laces up for you."

Praise like this, for a child at any age, is not healthy, real, or sustainable. It is plainly misleading. To be effective praise must communicate that each of us connect to family, or our class group, through genuine efforts and contributions.

So, how might delivering praise look in real life? There is an "easy to replicate" style to this. When you catch a child doing something you like or value, jump in, and give them some positive feedback, just a word or two. This way, they know they are on track, and can repeat the skill that is being used! At home for instance, imagine nine-year-old Zac has dragged out the dreaded monopoly set and is setting it up on the lounge room floor. You can hear him trying to convince his seven-year-old brother, Jett, to play with him because it will be fun. Your experience shouts from the roof tops that they never last longer than 20 minutes and it always ends badly! So, you keep an eye on them and remain tuned into their interaction. Then, ten minutes into game you deliberately walk through the lounge room. As you pass the boys, looking busy, you deliver a compliment, *"Boys I love the way you're playing together. Zac? Great leadership!"* Then you walk away. However, you continue to monitor the state of play and in another ten minutes you might sit with the boys and praise both for working together so well. By catching and commenting on the positive interactions, you have highlighted that you value their cooperative skills and best efforts. Often, it is no more than developing the skilful "art" of catching a child doing something worthy, smiling, and pointing it out. This design is so much more proactive than allowing the boys to tire, stumble, and end up with the inevitable argument.

The behavioural experts say we should make five to ten remarks that capture the positive moments for every one comment that redirects behaviour or does not shine optimistically on a child. Wow! I think that is a goal likely to be attained by saints and angels. Seriously, a ratio of three to one, and being conscious of this ratio, is perfect. As with all things, it is the *balance* that counts.

So often, the young person that looks as though they least appreciate our connection and praise is the one who aches for it. At school, it is the trickier students who need to hear your private encouragement most often. They are the ones who most feel overwhelmed, underperforming, or hopeless in a school environment. As well, given the conflict that often bubbles away in their life it is easy for them to feel unwanted and ready to react. My plea is to be resourceful and find ingenious ways to build credit with the harder to reach child. Make it your mission and behold the changes. Never stop trying to connect and build relationship!

Build your credit rating!

When I talk about building credit, I am focused on what we SAY and DO to bring our children and students closer to us. Building a solid credit history is not something that happens without intention and effort. The secret is to develop habits, routines, sayings, and opportunities that allow our credit rating to grow. Without a good credit rating, the rub caused in the trickier moments can rapidly spiral into yet another crisis. By building credit, we also build a trusting relationship to work within, and in turn, they have enough faith in us to share or seek guidance when needed.

So, what do you SAY and DO to deliberately build credit and positive connections? One way to understand this is to answer this question, honestly: How long is it since you laid on the floor or on a bed with your child, whether they are young or older, and while staring at the ceiling happily chatted about a myriad of apparently pointless things? Such moments are priceless because they build trust and loyalty. This in turn offers protection to the relationship when it is tested.

Build your credit rating

ACTIVITY

What is it you do to remind them how precious your connection is?
What is it you say to remind them how much you love them?
A few ideas to connect and build credit with your children and/or students:

Things to DO

Ask them to help you with things.
Ask them to spend time with you.
Be curious about their life.
Chat more.
Smile more.
Cook and bake.
Find a hobby to do together.
Find a spot to be quiet together.
Get into a joint project.
Give backrubs and feet massages.
Give them your full attention.
Go for a drive or a road trip.
Go to events even when they say it doesn't matter.
High five more.
Hug more, even as they go through that wooden hugger stage as a teen.
Invite them into parts of your life they do not get to see.
Laugh more.
Learn a dance to dance together.
Learn a song to sing together.
Learn about their favourite music, food, friends, or anything!
Learn dad jokes together.
Learn to play their video games and sports.

Look at their baby and toddler pictures.
Make a joint music playlist.
Make paper airplanes.
Make times when you are silly and playful.
Make up a ridiculous story, then it's their turn.
Make up your own game.
Offer help.
Paint your toenails together.
Play board games.
Play card games.
Play chasey/tag.
Play good old fashioned hide and seek.
Provide time to listen and chat each night.
Share a book.
Share a journal.
Share a snack.
Talk about when they were little and why you love them so much.
Talk less, ask more questions, and listen more.
Tell them a true story, then it's their turn.
Walk and talk.
Watch a sunrise, a sunset, or stream a new series together.
When it is time, help them learn to drive.
Wrestle more.

And, while on things to do, why not embed "a group weather massage" into what you do to deliberately connect with each other at home or in the classroom. A group weather massage is a soothing activity to de-stress, and most children adore it! Simply arrange yourselves in a small circle, sitting on the floor, so each of you can reach the back of the person sitting in front of you.

Place the script below on the floor so you can read it. Ready? Let's begin…

Using a strong voice, begin the story: "Once upon a time there was a big yellow sun…"

Follow up with a gentler voice to give the instruction: "So, place one hand on the person's shoulder in front of you and use the other to firmly rub a large circle on their back to make the big beautiful yellow sun."

Strong voice: "The big yellow sun warmed the whole world."

Gentler voice to carry the next instruction: "With both hands draw warm sunrays coming from the sun by dragging your hands right across their back."

Strong voice: "Suddenly clouds appear in the sky and cover the big yellow sun."

Gentler voice: "Lightly rub small circles with the tips of your fingers all over their back."

Strong voice: "Then, the wind comes along and blows, harder and harder..."

Gentler voice: "Strongly rub circles onto the person's back with the heels of your hands."

Strong voice: "It builds and builds and the wind turns into a whirlwind."

Gentler voice: "With both hands begin at shoulders and make swirling 'twirling-strokes' and gradually work down the back."

Strong voice: "Then came the lightening."

Gentler voice: "Make zig-zaggy lightening run across their back with your fingertips."

Strong voice: "Now comes the thunder."

Gentler voice: "Pat both hands over and over, firmly, on their back."

Strong voice: "Next is the rain."

Gentler voice: "With both hands use fingers so it feels like rain running down their back."

Strong voice: "And, it rains harder and harder..." (Continue, and go faster)

Strong voice: "until the rain turns to hail."

Gentler voice: "Change your finger tip movement to quick but gentle poking of the back."

Strong voice: "Suddenly, the wind stops and is still. It begins to snow, and everything becomes blanketed in soft white snow."

Gentler voice: "Push and pat the back ever so lightly with open hands to show the snow gently falling. Keep going."

Strong voice: "The only thing to see was a black cat that climbed on to the roof of the house. She wanted to see what was going on. She was followed by her kitten, and by another and another."

Gentler voice: "Make one hand climb from lower back up to the shoulders just as if it were a cat climbing up on to the roof. Once your hand reaches their shoulder roll it over from 'palm' to 'back of hand' as if one of the cats were flopping down to rest. Do one cat at a time. Remember, there are four cats to jump up altogether!"

Strong voice: "Finally, the fog appears. Everything remains still and quiet."

Gentler voice: "Lay both hands flat on their upper back and press hard."

Strong voice: "Then, the big yellow sun comes back out. It burns the cold fog away and warms up the Earth once again so everyone can go about their day."

Gentler voice: "As in the beginning, place a hand on one shoulder and use the other to rub a large circle on the back to make the big yellow sun."

Author unknown, but thank you for this chance to connect and reconnect with our children.

Things to SAY

"Can I have a hug?"

"Can we go together?"

"Can you teach me how to...?"

"Have a good day! See you!"

"How did you think of that?"

"How do you feel about that?"

"I am so thankful that you are in our family!"

"I believe in you."

"I have faith in you."

"I know you can handle it."

"I like you and that's really different to loving you."

"I love spending time with you."

"I love you just the way you are."

"I love you."

"I'm excited about doing this with you!"

"I'm proud of you."

"I'm proud to be your mum/dad."

"I'm ready to listen."

"I'm sorry. How can we fix this?"

"Let's try it your way."

"Love you to the moon and back and more."

"Shall we start over again?"

"Tell me more."

"Tell me. What can I do to be a better parent?"

"That was thoughtful of you."

"What challenge or project could we take on together?"

"Will you forgive me?"
"You are a good friend. To me and others."
"You are kind."
"You make me smile."
"You were right."
"You're not meant to be perfect. None of us are!"
"You're special to me."

What we SAY and DO plays a vast part in shaping our children's picture of the world, of themselves and their future. I can still hear my mum's encouraging words whenever I am challenged by something or when a new opportunity arises – *"If you don't give it a go, you'll never know!"* and *"Don't die wondering."* Her voice tone, words, and confidence in me remain with me to this day.

Three special questions

I challenge you, as a parent, to find the right moment and ask your children these questions:

1. What do I SAY and DO that tells you I love you, and want the best for you?
2. What do you SAY and DO that shows you want the best from our relationship?
3. What do we SAY and DO that that upsets or harms our relationship, sometimes?

Next, I challenge you, as an educator, to find the right moment and ask your students a similar set of questions:

1. What do I SAY and DO that tells you I want the best for you?
2. What do you SAY and DO that shows me you want the best from our relationship?
3. What do we SAY and DO that that upsets or harms our relationship, sometimes?

These three questions will build your credit rating with both your children and students. They will hear your desire to improve your relationship. Be brave and do it!

Cultivate those blossoming character strengths

Whether we truly appreciate it or not, all young people in our care look to us to endorse the compassionate or humane qualities we see in them. This helps them to feel as though they belong, are worthy, and can contribute. Think about it. Each of your children and students has unique qualities or character strengths, such as fairness, open-mindedness, sincerity, gentleness, reliability, likability, persistence, intelligence or wisdom, determination, lovingness, loyalty, honesty, humour, or kindness. It is our job to awaken these attributes and help them evolve.

So, when chatting with them, make a point to use adjectives that highlight unique qualities you see in them. Given that their self-awareness and self-image are still emerging, it is such a boost in confidence for a child to know the precious strengths a teacher, parent, grandparent, auntie, or uncle sees in them. Make it a mission to be able to automatically say three, four, or five of these uniquely personal assets emerging in each of your children. Keep them on the tip of your tongue ready to be used! Let them walk away from a conversation thinking, *"Wow! My dad sees me as a loyal and sensitive soul."* What a sincere way to enhance their budding identity!

Review on the STAR ACT – praise

- Make your praise about the behaviour, process, or effort.
- Keep it honest, warm, and concise.
- When you are pleased with a young person's efforts, please say so.
- Small, ongoing positive comments have a cumulative effect on children's self-image and confidence.
- Aim to praise the small changes, wins and successes, rather than waiting until your child has reached perfection.
- Never let a day pass without saying a few words of encouragement.

- Use non-verbals to praise: a thumbs up, smile, tousle of the hair, or high five are honest and easy ways to show you are impressed by a behaviour or an effort.
- We praise children because it helps to build their pride and a desire to cooperate.
- Make your praise appropriate. For example, teens often appreciate praise delivered privately, whereas younger children respond beautifully to being singled out.

10

ONE SIZE does not fit all

An alternative

I am changing direction and raising an approach that is often poorly understood and maligned by parents and teachers. It is the skilful use of token economy systems.

Firstly, I'm compelled to raise the broader issue about appreciating our children's individual needs. Increasingly, we are accepting the harmful effects of forcing a neurodivergent thinker to conform precisely to a neurotypical style of thinking. Specifically, this includes young people with Autism, ADHD, and Learning Disabilities such as Dyslexia, Dyspraxia, Dysgraphia and Dyscalculia and so on. When we thoughtlessly apply strong pressure to conform, it will heighten anxieties and lead to confusion about one's identity and value. So, whether it's introducing a token economy system, anything at all, children must be treated with respect, kindness, and thoughtful consideration about their style and capabilities.

I reject any system where there is a fixation on rewards for so-called success and disapproval for falling short. When we choose approaches grounded in understanding, connection and relationship, we give ourselves the freedom to develop new skills in the context of meeting a child's emotional needs.

In a perfect world, our kids would always be keen to listen and do what we ask. In a perfect world, children would not need reminders, would not need to be held accountable, and we would never need to offer inducements, incentives, and rewards. In a perfect world, we would explain to them why a new task, new routine, or a new behaviour mattered. We would show them how to do it, and they would do it. When you think about it, this is the gold standard approach that we all aim for, and remarkably, sometimes we achieve it.

In the real world, here's how you might use the gold standard approach at home. Let us use the example of cleaning teeth because it causes a lot of

DOI: 10.4324/9781003346715-10

friction and hiccups for parents with kids aged anywhere from 4 to 16 years. In a relaxed moment you might say to your child, "Hey, how come you always get grouchy about cleaning your teeth every evening?" You might cuddle them, pull them closer to you, and listen. In this moment you try to understand how they really feel about it and assess their obstacles and difficulties. You warmly validate their feelings. You help them come up with a new option to approach the task a little more productively. You promise to help them rather than find fault with them. Then you mention, *"Hey? You do know why I'm keen for you to brush your teeth every day?"* And the image you show them on screen is one you downloaded earlier of some very neglected teeth with awful black decay. *"Yes,"* you say, *"I love you too much to let your teeth get to this point."*

Many children and teens will respond beautifully to this approach because they can feel your genuine support. And they have the capacity to think and work from an internal standpoint. This does not mean they will, from now on, and forever, clean their teeth twice a day, and perfectly. However, being able to respond from an intrinsic perspective sets the stage to give it a go!

Some children, however, cannot operate intrinsically, yet. For all kinds of reasons, their development is different, delayed, or problematic. They get side-tracked by single-mindedness, by distractibility, or by contrary reactions. These may be caused by immaturities, anxiety, "diverse abilities," sickness, or from a trauma-based past. Consequently, the gold standard approach, you know, the beaut one you wish you could use, is compromised for you. My advice is to park the gold standard approach for now, and try it from time to time, because it is likely to become the best approach down the track!

This is a tricky place to be as a parent or teacher because you know that what works for most other children does not work for yours, just yet. Your child is still reliant on help from the outside; incentives, enticements, motivators, rewards, pay-offs, and coaxing. Now is the time to trial a token economy system (Psynso, 2021). You might also know them as "star charts" or "reward charts" and think they are for young children. They can, however, be designed respectfully for older children and adolescents. Many, many educators around the world subscribe to ClassDojo (www.classdojo.com). This is a digital style token economy system that educators use to inspire positive behaviour and improved academic outcomes for students. Besides ClassDojo it is worth considering Classcraft, Classlink, Kinderpedia, and Seesaw.

Despite the unfair press token economy systems have received at times, they offer a dynamic kick-start for the kids who do not yet have well-developed powers of concentration, perseverance, and gratification delay. They offer the capacity to improve children's engagement, cooperation, and achievement. They are powerful because they allow children to see they can get it right, hear praise, and feel successful. Token economy systems also help us to remain positive and use proactive language.

Yet you will notice a few of your friends will harshly judge you when you raise this as an option. They roll their eyes in disapproval when they see the star or reward chart you have set up on the fridge for your child or teen. In addition, you read newspaper articles by Saturday and Sunday morning parenting experts that say kids do the right thing if their parents have a decent relationship with them. That makes you feel even shabbier. This judgement is unfair, sanctimonious, and damaging.

Others will tell you that if you use a token economy system you will turn your kids or students into "reward junkies" where they will always expect a pay-off for everything they do, and forever more! However, you realise that if their intrinsic motivation was better developed, you would be seeing them use it a lot more. You have learnt a tough lesson that misses many who are quick to criticise. The lesson you have learnt is that there is room in your toolbox for both systems, and it is a sorry mistake to believe there is always just one way to go about things. You know where you want to end up. You want to end up using the gold standard approach, but in the meantime, you are smart enough to use a token economy system as a temporary bridge to get to where you want to end up. You have my deep admiration. One size does not fit all, and you are displaying intuitiveness, flexibility, and positivity.

Creatively meet your child's needs

I remember a father wanting to set up a token economy system to support his 12-year-old son to implement a new idea. The idea was to put away his freshly washed clothes into his drawers and cupboards each week. Straight up his son said "no" to star charts and to rewards, because he didn't need a reward and didn't want a big deal over it. He opted for his dad to write it in his journal when he achieved the task each week. He set a personal goal over six weeks. They did it his way for six weeks, and it stuck! In essence, his 12-year-old son put his own stamp on a token economy system, and this helped him own it.

A few ideas to help you successfully run a token economy approach

1. Once you set it up, use it optimistically every day, and have a finish date. It is best to target just one behaviour you want to develop at a time.
2. Focus on positive language that coaches, skills, and guides your child to success. *"Hey, Braydon? Once you've cleaned your teeth you can put another sticker on your star chart."* This is so much better than standing in front of Braydon's star chart screaming, *"I'm over you Braydon! If you don't clean your bloody teeth right now, I'm ripping two stickers off!"*
3. Young children respond best to immediate feedback/incentives and older children can have longer delays built in between behaviour and reinforcement.
4. Make the incentive the child is working towards powerful. Tap into their currency.
5. Token economy always fails for kids who get whatever they want and whose parents allow them to control it.
6. Occasionally, as you catch behaviour you value, provide surprise reinforcement. Something above and beyond their expectation! It may be spending time together doing something you both enjoy.
7. Never take away privileges already earned. You may have to apply an educative consequence instead (see Chapter 8), and it will simply take them longer to achieve the goal.
8. Allow yourself to give reminders because many children cannot anticipate the future. Our planning must do this for them.
9. Token economy systems lose appeal over time. So, we need to be on our game by sometimes resting them, and constantly changing the style to keep interest and motivation!
10. Finally, you will not build reward junkies by using token economy systems because you are smart enough to fade the system over time.

Finally, here are six differing styles of token economy systems to whet your appetite.

Yes jars

ACTIVITY

Buy a large plastic jar for each of your children. Have them decorate the jar with their name on it. Every so often, perhaps once or twice a week, put coloured plastic tokens (each child can have their own colour) on the bench next to the jars. Tell the kids that during this hour you want to see smiles, hear "Yes, mum" or "Yes, dad" and see their helpful behaviours. Promise that each time you see a positive effort you will get them to place a token in their jar. Then, at the end of the hour they can add up the number of tokens they have received. Set up a menu that shows them what 5, 10, 15, or 30 tokens can be traded for. Allow them to save tokens from one time to the next so they can earn the more impressive incentives.

Red-hot ticket giveaway

ACTIVITY

Giving away raffle tickets that can later be collected in return for prizes is a fun way to motivate all children. When executed with skill it works delightfully with teens as well. Negotiate how many tickets the kids must collect to earn specific rewards. Bring out the red-hot ticket giveaway menu when you are ready to start. Tickets are handed out when tasks are completed on request – getting ready for school on time, when chores are done, saying "yes," getting into pyjamas without help, getting off a screen when asked, remembering to clean teeth, and so on. Give away plenty of tickets and make sure that lots of tickets need to be collected to win the more desirable rewards. The red-hot ticket giveaway only lasts for one hour, every so often. This sparkling approach can lift the mood and acknowledges persistence.

STAR CHARTS: Using a "magical mystery tour" as a reward

ACTIVITY

Sharon (my wife) and I are not sure where this idea came from, but we used it when our girls were of primary school age. When either of the girls achieved a target that we had set together we organised a family day out that involved visiting a series of surprise places. These "magical mystery tour days" always proved to be joyful. Today, our children are women, but their magical mystery memories are still heart-warming. They are both sure that they did almost anything to have one of these days every so often. My recollection is not the same as theirs, but these reward days provided us with leverage toward influencing the behaviours we were chasing.

To monitor progress, we used a visual approach. In truth, any visually creative idea serves the purpose: gauges, clocks, thermometers, photographs of high-rise buildings where stickers can be placed on windows as a child works to master the target behaviour. The potential is limitless. Always place the chart where it can be easily seen. Ideal places are on the fridge, on the bedroom door, the family pin-up board or on their desk. Each morning, afternoon, or day ask them to place a sticker, a colour, a tick, or whatever has been negotiated on the chart.

Smiley face collecting

Smiley face collecting aims at strengthening positive experiences and cooperative behaviours. To start, purchase a few sheets of smiley face stickers. Discuss with one, or all your children, a particular behaviour you want to see more of. Every time you catch this behaviour in action stick a smiley face sticker into a grid. Start small with just a few gridded spaces and gradually build them up. At the end of the day, or week, count up the smiley faces they have earned. If they have been successful by achieving the predetermined number, then the reward you arranged together is achieved. If they have fallen short by not filling the grids, they continue on until done! It is a simple approach and can be varied to suit different age groups and interests. It helps to highlight that we are on their side as they create behaviours that work so much better.

Cut-ups!

To encourage cooperation and persistence try this. Your children will always want something. So, next time when they ask, and you know that they will get it sooner or later, simply say, "yes." Then, go to a device together and order it online. Next print out an image of what you have just ordered and cut it into 10, 12, or 15 pieces. Now it resembles a jigsaw puzzle. Name one valuable behaviour you would like to see them use each day. Make it specific and be prepared to positively support them so they can find success. Each day they are successful they achieve one piece of the puzzle. When they have collected all the pieces, what you ordered online is theirs. This strategy has great scope to be adapted!

A clever point system

Ten-year-old Louis and his mum devised a point system which inspired him to contribute more around the house. Each day Louis could earn 1 point for feeding the dog, 1 point for making his bed, 2 points for stacking the dishwasher, 2 points for picking up the doggy doo, and 2 points for taking out the recyclables. Louis needed to achieve 30 points to achieve a "Hot Wheels car." They were his obsession. Diane was clever and deliberately whetted his appetite with a brief visit to the store where Louis saw the entire set. In the ensuing weeks Dianne was happy to prompt Louis, but the beauty of their simple system was the way it dramatically reduced his resistance. It required little effort to maintain and monitor, as largely Louis could be left to record the points on the sheet taped to the fridge. It was a win/win solution and with so many cars to collect it took Louis several years. In the end, he was doing it for fun.

To finish up, I am compelled to write something real, that reflects the inexplicable twists and turns of life. What happens when a token economy system does not work? Does this mean you and your best efforts have miserably failed? Have you wasted your time?

No, this is not the case. Sometimes when token economy methods are researched and beautifully implemented, they will fail. Once the reward is achieved, things go right back to square one. At other times, the token economy system gets swallowed up in the melee of family or classroom life. Sometimes, even though the adults and the children enthusiastically agree on an approach and an incentive, it fizzles. Sometimes kids find them outright embarrassing.

The most important thing is the lessons learnt along the way. As I have mentioned many times, "this is all a beautiful messy work in progress," and there are no guarantees. The one guarantee is the amazing diversity in our children, and this means what works once or twice may not work consistently over time. What works for one child may not work for another. It reinforces that our children walk to the beat of their own drum, their own beautiful personality. And we need to respect this and respond appropriately.

11 WISE-GUIDES and SELF-CARE

I have written relentlessly about the significance of parents and educators being healthy (not perfect) role models to children, especially in the trickier moments. This is because it is from the behaviour of significant adults that children start to settle on their own values and identity – who they *can* become or who they *never* want to be. Largely, it is from parents that children embrace a blueprint for living either a healthy, satisfying life, or a life beset with troubles, drama, and discontent. What we have learnt is that the lessons we teach our children are mostly from our actions.

In this chapter, I turn the focus from children to us, the adults. I intend to delve into two realms. Both are connected to safeguarding your best physical and emotional health, because every day your kids and students need you to be well and in the right frame of mind to connect, and truly lead them.

Firstly, who are your wise guides or role models?

Who are the people that keep you grounded, inspired, motivated, and sane?
Who energises you? Who encourages you?
Who are the people that have your back?
Who checks in on you?
Who is cheering for you?
Who helps you to become the best possible version of yourself?

Secondly, let us explore how you look after yourself? What have you put in place to care for yourself, to find happiness and experience moments to recover and feel renewed?

DOI: 10.4324/9781003346715-11

Who are the people that keep you encouraged and switched on?

Please grab a pencil and paper. From the middle of the page draw three concentric circles. Place your name in the middle because a sensible start is to surround yourself with those who are doing a similar journey to you.

Sometimes the most powerful influences in life are those who are already in it. They know your history, understand it, want to walk with you, and are not likely to be critical or dismissive.

In this first space out from you, place a name, or names of those who have your back and you totally trust. It may be your mother or father, a sibling, auntie, uncle or cousin, a friend, a neighbour, a work colleague, or a likeminded acquaintance who you see regularly and can bare your soul to.

Now move out to the next space. The person or people's names you put here may not be as close, but you know they have an investment in your life.

Next to each name write what it is you receive and value from each of them? Each person can bring different skills and competences into your life. What you're doing is surrounding yourself with a few grounded friends. Physically, this is what your support network looks like.

Establishing this kind of network is powerfully healthy, perhaps lifesaving. It's more than alright to ask for help and to expect it from the right people. And when it is offered, please accept it, because help comes from a place of love. Do not be scared to lean on the right people. Most of all, role models or wise guides are there to listen, to exchange ideas, without judgement. Their goal is to help light the way for you. They will validate that this parenting thing is tough and emotional support is a must, not a luxury. They will also tell you that parenting alone, or parenting a child or children with a disability, or parenting three children under five years of age, is even tougher.

This is the moment to introduce my three wise guides. So much of my child-centred appreciation has emanated from these people over the years.

My first wise guide: Hiam Ginott

Hiam Ginott was born in Israel in 1922 and spent most of his life in the USA. Initially, he trained as a teacher, then retrained to become a psychologist. He was an iconic parent educator and wrote several best sellers, *Between Parent and Child, Teacher and Child: A Book for Parents and Teachers*, and *Between Parent and Teenager*. There are parallels between Hiam and the great artist, Picasso.

Picasso co-founded the Cubist movement. A way of looking at the world and turning it into an artistic expression that was almost counterculture at the time. His paintings went on to become models for a new generation of painters. In the same light, Hiam pioneered communication techniques that explicitly taught us how to listen and speak with young people offering a deeper respect and dignity, even though it was largely counter to the culture at the time.

Hiam Ginott on YouTube:

Haim Ginott 1 – www.youtube.com/watch?v=csj04h3zpFo
Haim Ginott 5 – www.youtube.com/watch?v=qx0XyTyOi8g
Haim Ginott 7 – www.youtube.com/watch?v=sMo80A_AAEw
Haim Ginott 8 – his wife, Alice – www.youtube.com/watch?v=5GFaCOh6Nps
Haim Ginott 10 – www.youtube.com/watch?v=a1OkD6jYq3k
Treat children like guests | Haim Ginott – www.youtube.com/watch?v=yFsB7
    ICQp3Y
Haim Ginott (play all) – www.youtube.com/playlist?list=PLRC2zHdRDOlU
    wjaxDYgE2buo9Qn6TrMFL

My second wise guide: Rita Pierson

Sadly, Rita died soon after her TED talk in 2013. She started teaching in 1972 and taught at all levels. She was a special educator, counsellor, an assistant principal, and a keen advocate for students from disadvantaged backgrounds. Watch her TED talks and adore her dry, wicked humour; be inspired by her deep humane spirit! Keep an ear out for her unique marking system. I embrace it. When a student got 18 questions wrong out of 20, she put "plus 2" on his assignment with a BIG smiley face. She says, "2 out of 20 sucks all the life out of you, "plus 2" gives you something positive to work from." I admire the value she places on relationships. How the simple act of being an authentic champion for a child, whether you are a teacher, parent, auntie, uncle, or friend, can shine brightly with a child, now and into their adulthood.

Rita Pierson on YouTube:

Every kid needs a champion | Rita Pierson – www.youtube.com/watch?v= SFnMTHhKdkw

Rita Pierson: School Starts at 8 – www.youtube.com/watch?v=Lju4BweO7z Q&list=PLZVAdKORbYZyKkowQ40r5YAgGEBWKDhVo

Rita Pierson: What about Jack? – www.youtube.com/watch?v=QwdtjlN818o &list=PLZVAdKORbYZyKkowQ40r5YAgGEBWKDhVo&index=3

I am certain that Rita's humanistic approach was aroused by the work of Carl Rogers. Carl Rogers (1902–1987) was an American psychologist and one of the founders of the "positive psychology" movement. He believed that for a person to "grow" they needed a situation that offered truth, care, acceptance, and empathy. He assumed that without these, relationships and healthy personalities do not develop well. Carl Rogers' thoughts have made many memorable quotes. For a few of these try – www.azquotes.com/ author/12540-Carl_Rogers

Carl Rogers on YouTube:

Carl Rogers on Person-Centered Therapy Video – www.youtube.com/watch? v=o0neRQzudzw

A Conversation with Carl Rogers: The Job of a Therapist | Saybrook University – www.youtube.com/watch?v=cabN4yE2fZo

Carl reminds us, whether we are a parent at home or an educator in a school setting, that a trusting relationship, poised modelling, the teaching of skills, and a few well-placed strategies to engineer a safer environment are all we've got! Thank you, Carl!

My third wise guide is New Zealand's current Prime Minister, Jacinda Ardern

Born July 26, 1980, Jacinda became leader of the New Zealand Labour Party in 2017 and the country's youngest prime minister in more than 150 years. She displays the quintessence of assertiveness, a stunning blend of optimism, composure, strength, leadership, and kindness. I want to stress this combination – notably the virtues of strength and kindness. Traditionally these have been viewed as contrasting virtues sitting at virtually opposite ends of the leadership spectrum! In other words, to lead with kindness was interpreted as a weakness. Kindness and strength were viewed as mutually exclusive, so a good leader must be strong above all else. Nothing could be further from the truth.

She also became a feminist role model when an interviewer quizzed her on whether she planned to have children in October 2017. She answered the question to that journalist's satisfaction. The next day, another journalist took her to task. They suggested that employers had a right to know whether prospective female employees planned on taking time off from work to have children. It was in this moment that she responded with real strength and kindness saying, *"It is the woman's decision about when they choose to have children. It should not predetermine whether or not they are given a job or have opportunities."*

In August 2019 Sky News host, and radio shock Jock, Alan Jones disagreed with Jacinda Ardern's comments about Australia taking more responsibility for climate change in the Pacific region. He said, someone should *"shove a sock down her throat"* to silence her. Subsequently he apologised for what he termed a "clumsy remark." Her response displayed kindness, strength, and humour. Ms Ardern said she doesn't *"have an opinion on every single person who says something about me"* and that she'd get *"revenge"* on Mr Jones on the rugby field. *"I understand that (Jones) of course used to be closely linked to the Wallabies… let's just say that I think revenge is best served through a Bledisloe Cup,"* she said. So, the next time you face a challenging moment with your child, try channelling Jacinda Ardern's keenly developed assertive skills. She reminds us that authentic grown-ups avoid the fight and drama. The real fight is within us, and it is a fight to remain kind and consistent. To state what has happened and what needs to happen, but to stay emotionally connected and lead with poise.

My early wise guides

Finally, thank you to Mary, Mavis, and Ruth. I met you in those first few precious years of teaching. I was 23 years old, bright eyed and bushy tailed, and a total novice. You could tell, so the three of you conspired to take me under your collective wings. I didn't know what you were doing to me, but in truth, I had little idea about what I was doing anyway. I did not appreciate the scope of your gift at the time. Thank you because you reshaped my thinking about children, childhood, child development, and teaching in classrooms. You gave me a most precious framework called "child-centred teaching" where I learnt how to place the child, their emotional and learning style, needs, and ambitions, at the centre of the learning experience. Your gift has stuck with me forever. How lucky was I?

It is to our advantage to draw inspiration from a wise guide and channel their energy into our thoughts, habits, and actions. As well, surround yourself with sensible friends (not perfect ones) who appreciate you and may be dealing with similar complexities in their lives. Such wise guides are invaluable!

How do you look after yourself?

ACTIVITY

What have you put in place to care for yourself? What is it you do to deliberately buoy your happiness and emotional recovery? While we are busy supporting our children to grow emotionally, physically, spiritually, and in every way that matters, most of us do not actively look after ourselves. Yet, we know this lack of self-care is detrimental in the longer term to our health and wholehearted commitment. In his book *A Fearless Heart: How the Courage to Be Compassionate Can Transform Our Lives*, Thupten Jinpa describes self-care as the ability to be frequently kind to ourselves. Failure to lay this foundation results in being unable to give to others and is likely to lead to poor health. He uses the parallel of being on a plane and putting your oxygen mask on first before attempting to help another (Jinpa, 2015).

So, how do you take care of your mental and physical health?
How do you show kindness to yourself?
What do you do to nourish yourself and recuperate?
Have you, or someone close to you, had a physical or a mental health scare and now realise how precious self-care is?
Do you have a self-care plan?

In principle, what I am talking about here is developing your own personalised mental health care plan. When we're fatigued, exhausted, or fed up, the natural tendency is to grab at the POWER-OVER and restrictive techniques.

We pull back on relationships, get snippy and short-tempered, become emotionally distant, and strengthen rules and consequences. We bunker down, shrink into ourselves, and try to survive. We only do what we absolutely must. That's right. You guessed it. This is when we move away from the AUTHORATATIVE to the NEGLECTFUL quadrant (revisit Chapter 2, Which QUADRANT reflects your PARENTING or TEACHING style?).

Many of the remarkable parents and educators I work alongside resolutely support children who have elevated needs. They have children with "diverse abilities," although medically biased descriptors such as disabilities, disorders, deficits, conditions, and syndromes are more commonly used in the community. These amazing parents have taught me to take stock of the essentials first. Are you eating right, sleeping adequately, exercising or being active, and do you have a small community of friends and meaningful relationships around you?

It is intriguing how easily these absolute essentials can slip away from overcommitted parents. With a little resolve and a few tweaks, these can always be improved, and small improvements yield surprisingly positive results. Here are a few of the things my clients do to restore, invigorate, and recharge:

- Commit to time for fun with family and friends.
- Sing in a choir.
- Go hiking or bushwalking.
- Attend some kind of art or craft classes to let hidden talents and desires shine.
- Listen to music to escape.
- Join a book, gardening, movie, or breakfast club.
- Go to the gym.
- Walk each day, with or without the dogs.
- Eat right, more consistently.
- Regularly catch up with a dear friend for a coffee and chat, even if it is just once a fortnight.
- Book in regular treats like a haircut, facial, massage, manicure, or pedicure.
- Enrol in a new course to learn wood carving, belly dancing, cooking, leadlight or floral design, etc.
- Take a long soak in the bathtub to wash the worries away.

For the best chance to be optimistic and lead, we must create opportunities to find happiness and rejuvenation. Even small steps in this direction will help bring hope. There is no other way! Without developing and sticking to a conscious "self-care plan" our happiness, effectiveness, and emotional health are restricted. Do what you can to nourish yourself, recuperate, and revive. Never discount the fact that we have a choice. We can choose to be a part of a myriad of solutions, even if it is sitting on the edge of the bath once a day, just for 90 seconds, to celebrate the beauty within each of our kids.

Recollection by a parent: "Just for 90 seconds"

Sometimes there was not enough time in my day to look after myself. For a long while this is how it was. I had two children, intellectually gifted and with disabilities, and both were at different schools 20 minutes away in different directions through necessity. I was dealing with constant schooling problems, preparing individual meals for breakfast, lunch, and dinner because of astonishing sensory intolerances, a husband who worked long hours and was often away, no family help, the boys had constant colds and injuries, appointments with doctors and therapists, alongside hours of homework to help with every night. Life was tough going.

It's not that I didn't know better, it was that I could not do better. It hurt that I felt so overwhelmed and looked like a spoiling, controlling, ill-informed mother, with a dirty house, who cut corners everywhere. It was so hard.

For a long while I couldn't even find five minutes each day for myself. The best advice I got was to go to the bathroom, sit on the edge of the bath and take three deep breaths and think of the remarkably beautiful things my gorgeous boys bring. It was such an effort to find 90 seconds and it was the best I could do. It did help. The boys have grown, I have moved on, and life is so much better. Please draw strength from my story.

My friend, Amara

Recollection by a parent: "Write your thoughts down"

I find it helpful to write my thoughts down. I'll tell you why. It's because thoughts are invisible and once you see them on a screen, or on paper, it's a lot easier to assess them. I slide them around into categories and work out the ones that are truly in my control versus those that are not. Writing thoughts down and manipulating them in a physical way brings a clarity that over-thinking cannot. This helps me to accept there are some things I can't control. And, what about the things I can't control? Well, I have a special place for these. I put them into my "Fuck it bucket." So, I visualise myself picking up these thoughts and putting them into my "Fuck it bucket." I have been known to do this physically as well. That is, to write them down, rip them up and scatter them into a rubbish bin.

My friend, Niamh

CLOSE

12

Thoughts and reflections

Thank you for walking with me to build this practical and humane space where children can thrive. Whether you are a parent, educator, allied health professional, grandparent, foster parent, any kind of parent, auntie, uncle, or older cousin, it does not matter. What matters is how we connect to the children in our lives. By virtue of being an adult it has become our turn to step up and do the best we can to nurture a younger generation. It is our time to teach children the depth of being human and how to live generously in a community. To assure every child that they are beautifully unique and worth our every effort.

I chose to work from *that* moment when we must get involved, redirect, or call one of our children on an unsafe, careless, or selfish act because these are the trickiest of moments but are nonetheless real moments that occur continuously. Such moments should not be thought of as annoying, tedious, or infuriating. They happen in every home and classroom and they always happen for a reason. They arise because our children are inexperienced, learning, and bound to make mistakes. They happen because a young person is clumsily expressing an emotional need, and sometimes this need is based on a faulty logic or may be driven by an unrecognised traumatic event. This is our call to use the compassionate techniques – "soft eyes and a warm heart." Techniques that nurture a child's pride, free them from shame, and leave them in a position where they are more likely to want to make changes, rather than having their autonomy stolen and feeling gazumped by an adult yet again. On this, try to keep your preferred working

DOI: 10.4324/9781003346715-12

style in the forefront of your mind (revisit Chapter 2, Which QUADRANT reflects your PARENTING or TEACHING style?). Children need adult models to connect with and chat to, who will have their back and be a positive influence.

I hope we have walked far enough for me to deepen your appreciation about the emotion, and the need, that always sits under every kind of behaviour. Especially under "MIS"behaviour. Once we truly embrace the idea of thinking about why a behaviour may be happening, we receive the freedom to be a child's champion. To be their best coach, capable of showing love, grace, strength, while drawing a line in the sand during the trickiest of moments. If I have aroused a new mindset, or a new perspective in you, I am so happy. Now there is no turning back!

Please bear in mind that each of us are vulnerable learners. We have our learner's plates on too. Everything we do with our kids and students is for the first time, and because of this, we often feel there is an urgency and a lot at stake. Please be kind to yourself. Train yourself to take a few deep breaths as you enter a contentious moment. Slow down your natural inclination to quickly correct a child's behaviour and make the situation right, right now. Time is usually not of the essence, even though it may feel like it is. Nor is the essence making our children obedient. Obedience will come, but what I have offered in this book are foundation approaches where obedience grows from self-actualisation (gradually learning how to be the best version of oneself) rather than having obedience imposed.

To conclude, I reached out to current and past clients. Some are now in their 30s with children of their own. All are dear friends. I asked them to reflect on their early years and write something meaningful about their childhood, parents, the place of family, special teachers, and school memories. I have done this because when caught up in the chaos of life it is hard for us to see "the forest for the trees." My hope is their reflections inspire you to take heart and appreciate the beautiful and deep lingering influences you are creating. What you are doing is building an eternal bond with a child. I imagine this bond as a bridge. It is a gift for life because they will be enticed to cross it, back and forth, over and over, to collect and carry the wisdom and humanity you offered as a parent, teacher, or significant other. In turn, they will take these virtues, and more, into their adult lives and use them freely, with a new generation of young. Your love, care, and guidance has allowed them to become their own connected person who wants to attach to others and continue this beautiful thing we call humanity.

Enjoy what follows, as their insight offers clarity. It reassures us of the benefits that arise from communicating using this precious technique.

Nothing is more important to me than my family. Some days we can't stand each other, then on other days we long to reunite. My family, especially mum who did it by herself, put me first and asked for nothing in return. I wouldn't be half the person I am this very day without her. When I was growing up my goal was to represent my country in my chosen sport, so my mum worked tirelessly to make sure I had every opportunity. She left me with the values of love, loyalty, compassion, commitment, and an amazing work ethic. Thanks mum!

Jordan Biggie Steffens, 33 years
www.facebook.com/Jordan.celticwarrior.Steffens

Within the first few weeks of Year 9, applications were open for house captain. Whilst I had interest in applying, I decided not to bother as I didn't think I had a chance. My new home-room teacher walked with me one morning only barely knowing me. He was so encouraging. I listened and grasped that he saw something in me I never saw in myself. He gave me the courage to do it. I got the house captain position and continued to apply for leadership positions the years that followed. I have never been an incredibly confident person, but his open-heartedness and belief in me truly changed the way I viewed myself.

Georgia, 19 years

Traumatic teenage years accumulated. My anxiety started to perceive success as something unattainable because of potential risks, "What if I don't get an A?" "What if it's not perfect?" A teacher pulled me aside one day and said, "Every night I want you to imagine the different moments of your hopes coming true." Not only did this help me to fall asleep but the positive thoughts seemed to accumulate into positive thoughts throughout each day. By the time I got to Year 12 my perspective and academic achievements had vastly changed. What I did appreciate, and will never forget, is the few minutes that teacher took to change my life. Grateful – forever.

Candace, 30 something

My family is made of two lots of parents because my parents split up early. Family is my "safe place" where I can be me. It's the place we make happy memories that I can carry with me.

My mum has done lots of extra special things for me but the biggest one is making sure that I still see my dad even though he doesn't live near us and I know that's been hard for her. I used to believe that mum was the reason that they broke up but this year I worked out that wasn't the case. I realised that mum made lots of sacrifices for me and was actually being kind to me until I was old enough to understand what had happened and why.

Mum always helped me when things were tricky. One of her best ideas was to see Mark. He gets me, understands me, and helps me to improve – it's like he is part of my family too!

One of my happiest memories I often think of is when I was little mum had a two-door convertible car. She would take the roof off and we would drive along singing songs really loudly – it was heaps of fun!

Noah, 12 years

Slowly, painfully slowly, we learned to appreciate our individual quirks, failings and traits that make up the untidy sum of our family. Now I'm doing it again, this time as a mum with my own children and spouse.

Sophee, 30 something

My Mum is excellent and nice. She makes me breakfast and helps me do homework. I work with Dad in the shed helping him build stuff. I love that.

Lucas, 9 years

My family? They're my rock. Mum and Dad have always loved me regardless of my questionable decisions. They were able to separate me from my sometimes "not so good" behaviour.

Today, they are my lifelong friends. It was a slow transition. A slow burn from being the rule-makers to the people who know me and want to know me. I now have conversations with them about the latest political or COVID-19 debate, about anything. They are the only ones I feel comfortable asking how to properly poach an egg, again and again. They will listen to my endless rants, pause, consider, then be honest with me. Sometimes what they say is uncomfortable to hear, but who else shows me such honesty and love wrapped together?

I think the real contributor towards our positive relationship is the trust they have long put into me. With this trust came a desire to be responsible and accountable (which by the way, didn't harden up until later in my teenage years). I do not know how I would have survived through high school, and the highs and lows of adolescence, without them as strong presences within my life.

Lucy, 22 years

My Year 9 science teacher had a profound impact on me and my future. I recall her gentle disappointment with our chemistry results. She wanted us to do better, to give our best and not to settle on scraping by. I got a C and I knew I could do better. Her message was not about getting a higher grade. It was to be better. And the belief that someone believed I could do it, inspired a belief in myself.

What she does not know is that it stirred my love of science. Her care and words led me to study at university to obtain a PhD in Chemistry. Whilst I do not work in the field now, the skills I developed as a scientist help me every day; to look at things from an analytical perspective, and to question why. The dedication to complete a difficult course of study helped me in every aspect of life. I would love to be able to thank her; she changed the course of my life.

**Jo, a friend, 40 something. I'm also
blessed to mentor her boys**

My Mum makes me happy when she cuddles me and makes my favourite dinner, curry rice. Dad makes me happy when he makes me cheese pizza for lunch.

Daniel, 7 years

Recently, I was reminded of the preciousness of my family. I had just sat an exam that I had spent 9 months studying for. When my results arrived, I was disappointed. I had not achieved the result I wanted.

131

My family and friends would ask how the exam went and Mum or Dad would simply squeeze my hand or rub my back. I believed that this exam would define my future, so my parents sat me down over lunch to talk.

I saw the pain they shared with me. They had seen the many months of hard work, they had constantly supported me when the self-doubt became overwhelming, and they too had made sacrifices to help me achieve my dreams. However, the most memorable part of this conversation was when they told me they cared more about the type of person I am than any of my achievements. They told me that they had my back, regardless of what I was to do next.

To me, my parents are my best friends. They lead with kindness and strength and are not afraid to tell me I'm wrong or call me out when they think I could have been better. They share their life stories with me and through this, they let me know that it is okay to struggle and it is okay to not be perfect – because life itself is not. They feel all the highs and lows of life just as I do, as they are riding the rollercoaster of life right beside me.

I look forward to telling them stories about my day – the good, the bad and the funny because they have always loved me for who I am. They challenge me to be the best version of myself and they have helped shape me into the person I am today.

Issie, 17 years

When I was in primary school my mother was hospitalised many times. My brother was severely intellectually disabled and lived at home until he was eight years old. With hindsight, I now see that my sister and I were his carers. We would often have lunch in the convent with the nuns. They were so kind and a meal for us frequently arrived home for dinner.

Vicki, 30 something

My Mum is a good Mum and I sleep with her in bed. She's warm. My Dad has had surgery because he had a thing growing on his brain and he got stitches. He's grumpy right now and I'm not going to listen to him when he's angry.

Charlie, 5 years

My family is my rock and I always feel like I belong. We laugh, cry and celebrate together, and contribute to each other's emotional worlds. I cannot imagine a world without them.

I could never understand the meaning as a little kid, about why I should "always be learning." At the time, it never made sense because I thought I knew everything! But now, I realise that under-standing is one of the most important ideas in life. The need to learn never stops. Looking out for others, being kind and humble are Mum and Dad's key values. I think I have been infused with these and I'm grateful.

Ethan, 19 years

I am 18 years of age. I'm probably one of Mark's longest serving pro-jects. I'm challenged by cerebral palsy, dyslexia, and more recently severe clinical depression. High school was never a happy place for me. My differences were obvious and because of these I became a target for silent, sophisticated bullying, gossip, and humiliation. I never graduated into teen girl world. Yet, I was incredibly blessed to be surrounded by a few extraordinary teachers. My beloved Special Education Teacher always led the way. She became my biggest sup-porter, defender, and friend. Whenever necessary she went into battle for me, convincing teachers to see things in a different way, or to put in a little extra time and effort. She listened to all my fears, worries, disappointments and rants.

I am grateful to her, and the amazing teachers who saw my poten-tial, and cared for it. They did not judge me or write me off because of my differences. They fought for me when I could not fight for myself and because of their belief in me I managed a score of 90.45% in my final year of secondary school.

Steph, 18 years, my friend

What I didn't realise until years later was that my parents were fight-ing their own demons from each of their pasts while they were rais-ing my sisters and me. With hindsight, they were doing their best. I had an unplanned pregnancy. My parents were ashamed and angry. I set myself a new ambition and it was to love my children for who they were and never to ridicule and shame them as my parents had done to me.

Then, as the years went by, I realised, being a perfect parent was hard to do. I said things to my children that I now regret. Was I so different from my parents? Two years ago, my daughter unexpectedly became pregnant and I wondered if my parents would once again remind me of the shame I had put them through back when I became pregnant. But they didn't. Instead, they rejoiced with us. They couldn't wait to become great-grandparents. A new softness and desire to engage in this new chapter of family replaced the hardness of our previous relationship.

Sharleen, 50 something, daughter, mother, and grandmother to be

I am grateful to have such a loving family. They have always been here for me and for each other. They have shaped me into who I am and I'm okay with that. My family and I have been through ups and downs, but it's the little ordinary things that make me feel as though I count. Like organising birthday dinners for me over the years, and spending ages on helping me pass a level on a videogame that I got stuck on.

Max, 14 years

In Year 11 I was struggling. My family had imploded, and I felt like it was my responsibility to hold everything together. My English teacher, who had noticed that I was inconsistent with my homework, made times where I could sit with her in a peaceful place without any other distractions or demands so I could focus. I felt visible and permitted to be just a student. Nearly 35 years later I still am brought to tears when I think about those times of reprieve from my grim reality. They gave me hope and a belief that I was more than my family's rescuer.

Alison, 50 something

My perceptive Year 12 teacher offered this wise comment to a fellow student. In truth, it was directed at the whole class on the eve of our exams. She said, "Whatever happens in the exams, remember this. The sun will still rise the next day, life will continue, and it will be okay. I've never forgotten, and I've held this wisdom ever since.

Selina, 40 something

"Family – where life begins and love never ends." My husband, daughter and I all have this as a tattoo and when our son is old enough, he will most likely have it too.

Kylie, 30 something

I love my Mum and Dad. They love me back. I just love being home with them.

Harry, 8 years

My family is always there, but honestly, it is brutal sometimes. I don't always get along with Mum and Dad. We disagree on a lot of things like what I watch on TV, how much time I spend on YouTube, like all the chores I'm asked to do, even the number of potato chips I can eat!

I struggled through Year 7. That was a tough year. I thought I did my best, but my report said I failed everything but art. I kept it together until I got home. I locked myself in the bathroom and cried and cried. Mum comforted me. Both Mum and Dad helped me get through this bad time, and many other bad times.

It hasn't been easy for them because it's not easy raising a son who has autism. I know that they love me, everything, but they can get overwhelmed just like I get overwhelmed. No kid should ever have to go through life not being able to lean back on their parents. Mum and Dad mean everything to me.

Wil, 15 years

Mr K was one of my middle school teachers. He turned my life around. I was a clever kid, but rebellious and obnoxious. I would have dropped out of school, or got kicked out, if it wasn't for this man's understated involvement. He saw past my behaviour, read into my feelings, and attached to me. Looking back, I think he attached and inspired us all. We wanted to do our work, and wanted to do well, because he spoke to us like we mattered.

Laura, 40 something

In Year 12 I experienced an unforgettable trauma. Going to school became difficult. If it wasn't for the intuition and kindness of one teacher, I'm not sure I would have got through the year. Thanks to him and others, I received an Australia Day Award the following year for my achievements at school. Now, 20 years later, I am still thankful. The trauma has healed, and that teacher will never know what a difference their kindness and encouragement made to my life.

Rebecca, 30 something

Dad is funny, loving and hard working. Mum takes care of us all. My sister doesn't really come across as nice to me, but sometimes she's nice. My little brother is funny and always wants to spend time with me. My place in my family is the middle child.

Grace, 8 years

I've always loved horror movies, but for a long time never told my parents. I thought they would be upset with my choice. Finally, when I told them, they helped me find some great age-appropriate horror movies. This made me feel like I could tell them anything. And now I do.

Chris, 13 years

My family means a lot to me because they've made me who I am. If I ever feel worried, I always know that my family will be there to help. The values that my parents have left me with are – respect, kindness and resilience. I was given those values by growing up with great parents.

Rhylan, 14 years

My son started school this year and struggled, big time, with the transition. His anxiety came out of the blue and we had school refusal almost every day. This was particularly challenging because with COVID-19 restrictions, parents were not permitted on site. His teacher quickly discovered his love of dinosaurs! She began leaving a plastic dinosaur at the school gate so that he had something to look forward to and collect. He felt so special and enjoyed searching for them each day. He cherished telling his kind teacher what the dinosaur was called, and something about it, when he entered her class. I will be forever touched by her care, patience, and willingness to read each child in her class. My son has now adjusted to his new routine and no longer needs a dinosaur to enter school.

Trish, 30 something

My family means the world to me. But the extra, extra special thing they have done for my sister and I is the opportunity to travel overseas (prior to COVID-19). We are not a rich family and save hard to go over to England every two years to see my grandparents. We spend a fortnight away and visit one other amazing place on the way home such as Dubai, Singapore, and Hong Kong. The fact that Mum and Dad committed to this is so special. It's helped me learn about the world, about myself and built family memories that will last forever. I absolutely love my family.

Evan, 14 years

Family is my unbreakable. They get me. They are my foundation and a calm centre to retreat to when needed. They have gone into bat for me more times than I want to remember, and against some pretty heavy fire. I am blessed to have them as my "life-team," always looking out for me and offering guidance, not judgement. To those of you who have children battling learning, emotional or behavioural problems, I know what you're facing. I faced these with my parents too. My advice – "Let your love lift them high offering them a calm centre to retreat to."

Sam, 28 years

Growing up with a double learning disability has not been easy. It has shaken my confidence and resilience. After finishing my primary school, my education fell into a heap. Mum and Dad bravely made the call for me to start at a new school. On my first day at my new school Mum taped a big note on the inside of our front door. It said, "You've got this, girl." Do you know what? I did! Even though the note is getting old it's still there! I continue to look at it every day on the way to school. My parents have always supported and believed in me and that's why I quietly help others.

Hayley, 16 years

We have a foster son. Now he's at high school and is gradually finding himself and his way in life. The early years were rough for him and everyone. When he was 6 years, I remember the school calling me one morning and asking me to come and pick him up because he was having a "no, no, no, no" day. Usually, they handled things beautifully and would only call as a last resort. They showed patience, intuition and understanding. How blessed we were. His previous school suspended him 23 times in reception. Not surprisingly, he despised going to school. Even worse was that he hated himself for his angry interactions and became deeply confused and frustrated.

Vashti, 40 something

These days, my parents are two of my best friends who have guided me through the obstacles and celebrations of life.

I had a rough Year 12. Filled with stress and anxiety. My parents tried their hardest to support and reassure me, despite me shutting them off. Mum sat down with me and made a "study plan," and I immediately felt like things would be okay. I also remember telling my Dad during Year 12 that I felt like I had failed as a daughter. His response was "no matter what, you will never, ever be a disappointment to me or your Mum." Looking back, I don't know how I would have got through Year 12 without my parents.

As I have grown older, I have reflected upon how my parents are not perfect. My Mum isn't afraid to spam the "family group chat" with updates on her latest meal or exercise routine, and my Dad loves to force my sister and me into watching another one of his SBS documentaries. These weird quirks and imperfections make my parents even more lovable and I wouldn't want it any other way.

I love that my Dad often challenges me to view situations from the perspective of other people, especially during conflict. Although I have found this frustrating at times, it has taught me the value of empathising with others and to view the world beyond myself.

I really enjoy bonding with my parents. With my Dad, I love exploring new shows, movies, and plays together and I know he will always be up for a walk with the whippets, Mindy and Mike. With my Mum, our dinners are almost always extended by an hour or two because I'm seeking advice or we're reminiscing about "the good old days." It is special moments like these that will always bring me and my parents together.

My parents are my backbone and are the people who know me better than anyone else. They are the people who I thank for shaping my work ethic, empathy, accountability, and honesty. I know my Mum and Dad gave parenting all they had, and I think they did a pretty awesome job.

Juliet, 20 years

My family means everything to me. They adopted me when I was 10 months old and have given me lots of opportunities to help me grow into the 13-year-old I am today. They have taught me love, respect, and forgiveness, and carry me to find the best version of myself. They love me unconditionally.

Mum and Dad are fantastic role models, even when they say "no." When I was young, I really wanted a dog, but they told me I was too young to look after it, just yet. At the time I didn't like it, but when I turned 11, they got me a beautiful, smart, loving dog called Clancy.

Ava, 13 years

My son was in Year 3 and was not progressing academically, losing confidence, and withdrawing socially. His teacher had a highly competitive focus on reading levels and scooting through the glorified reading boxes. He was terribly shy, identified with dyslexia and this reading situation terrified him. In the end, our only choice was to move. His new teacher was amazing – warm and wise. She told him to forget about readers and reading levels, and just find books that were fun and answered his curiosities. Very quickly he became a much happier boy, he wanted to read, wanted to go to school and had friends. He's now 18 years, enjoys reading and is a capable and independent learner. This teacher's insight and style was life-changing, and we are forever grateful.

Sharon, 40 something

Verse and prose on children and family

My wildlings

Be free my wildlings. Dance to the beat of your own drums, always.
Be you, no one in this world is like you.
Never be defined by people and their judgements; be bold, be
brave, and speak out, even when your voice shakes.
Be strong and courageous.

Learn how to decipher the truth. Truth has its own resonance.
Stand up for what's right, stand in your truth, even when it's hard.

Most of the time the easy road is the one that the crowd follows.
Have the tenacity and persistence to forge your own path.

Connect with your intuition, it will guide you like a powerful inner-compass that will align you with positive human connections and meaningful life experiences.

You will make mistakes and hit potholes in the road on your journey; recognise the hard moments or times as life-serving lessons that will encourage your minds, hearts and soul's expansion.
Always pick yourself up when you feel knocked down and move yourself forwards with the grit and grace you're made of.

I have your back.
No matter what, I'm behind you, and home will always be the place where you can safely express your big feelings and find peace in your pain.

It will always brim with love and acceptance, but also be the place where fair boundaries are taught, gratitude is practiced, and loving energy is exchanged.

My children, my wildlings, you are my biggest gifts and my most treasured teachers.
Jess, my friend

My family

My family is everything to me
By blood and by love
My family strengthens me
My family extends me
My family bends me
Always there to lend an ear
My family supports me with unconditional understanding
I have them to thank for all my success, my drive, my grit
My family facilitates my needs
They give me ability and remove my disability
Among them I feel normal

Accepted
I belong
Ross, thirty something

It's never too late

Now I am a grandmother I get another chance to lead with love and teach my sons, and grandchildren the precious lessons of being a family. It is never too late to learn and unlearn. Fortunately, the same opportunities to embrace your grown children and their children show up again and again.

I want you to know that you are loved and loveable. In our family we honour our stories of struggle and strength. We are gentle on ourselves and with each other, and we celebrate all the gifts that bring strength. I want you to watch me prepare, sometimes succeed, at other times fail, regroup, and try again with perseverance and patience. You will learn that self-love is not built on being selfless but through courageously asking for help.

In times of uncertainty, reach out to me. I cannot remove your pain, but we will cry and face the fears and grief, gently, quietly in the stillness and feel it all. At other times, we will laugh, sing, and dance, and give each other permission to revel in our glorious imperfections. No matter what, we will always belong here and to each other. In our vulnerability we will know joy.

This journey together holds many twists and turns, and the greatest gift is to live and love with your whole heart. Truly, deeply, I see you now as the sacred gift that now gifts me a new chance to teach, to learn, to love and live, in joy and with gratitude.
Tineke, mother to three and grandmother to eight

Welcome to Holland

I am often asked to describe the experience of raising a child with a disability – to try to help people who have not shared that unique experience to understand it, to imagine how it would feel. It's like this...

When you're going to have a baby, it's like planning a fabulous vacation trip – to Italy. You buy a bunch of guidebooks and make your wonderful plans. The Coliseum. The Michelangelo David. The gondolas in Venice. You may learn some handy phrases in Italian. It's all very exciting.

After months of eager anticipation, the day finally arrives. You pack your bags and off you go. Several hours later, the plane lands. The flight attendant comes in and says, "Welcome to Holland."

"Holland?!?" you say. "What do you mean Holland?? I signed up for Italy! I'm supposed to be in Italy. All my life I've dreamed of going to Italy."

But there's been a change in the flight plan. They've landed in Holland and there you must stay.

The important thing is that they haven't taken you to a horrible, disgusting, filthy place, full of pestilence, famine and disease. It's just a different place.

So you must go out and buy new guide books. And you must learn a whole new language. And you will meet a whole new group of people you would never have met.

It's just a different place. It's slower-paced than Italy, less flashy than Italy. But after you've been there for a while and you catch your breath, you look around... and you begin to notice that Holland has windmills... and Holland has tulips. Holland even has Rembrandts.

But everyone you know is busy coming and going from Italy... and they're all bragging about what a wonderful time they had there. And for the rest of your life, you will say "Yes, that's where I was supposed to go. That's what I had planned."

And the pain of that will never, ever, ever, ever go away... because the loss of that dream is a very very significant loss.

But... if you spend your life mourning the fact that you didn't get to Italy, you may never be free to enjoy the very special, the very lovely things... about Holland.

Emily Perl Kingsley

Series on children, parenting, and family

Anne with an E (2017)
Atypical (2017)
Big Little Lies (2017)
Big Love (2006)
Breeders (2020)
Everybody Loves Raymond (1996)
Kim's Convenience (2016)
Little Women (2019)
Modern Family (2009)
Odd Mom Out (2015)
Parenthood (2010)
Schitt's Creek (2015)
The A Word (2016)
The L Word (2004)
The Let Down (2016)
The Middle (2009)
This Is Us (2016)
Workin' Moms (2017)

Movies on children, parenting, and family

About a Boy (2002)
Bad Moms (2016)
Curly Sue (1991)
Father of the Bride (1991)
Hunt for the Wilderpeople (2016)
Instant Family (2018)
Kramer vs Kramer (1979)
Life as We Know It (2010)
Little Miss Sunshine (2006)
Marriage Story (2019)
Meet the Parents (2000)
Mr Mom (1983)
Mrs Doubtfire (1993)
Parental Guidance (2012)

Stepmom (1998)
The Castle (1997)
The Kids Are All Right (2011)
The Pursuit of Happyness (2006)
Together Together (2021)
What to Expect When You're Expecting (2012)
Where'd You Go, Bernadette (2019)
Yours, Mine and Ours (2005)

Documentaries on children, parenting, and family

7 Up (1984)
A Dangerous Son (2018)
Far From the Tree (2017)
Found (2021)
Louis Theroux Extreme Love – Autism (2012)
Louis Theroux's Transgender Kids (2015)
Minimalism (2021)
Miss Representation (2011)
Old People's Home for 4 Year Olds (2019)
Old People's Home for Teenagers (2022)*State of Play: Trophy Kids* (2013)
Still Loved (2016)
The Beginning of Life (2016)
The Mask You Live In (2015)
Unlocking the Heart of Adoption (2020)

Bibliography

Australian Bureau of Statistics (2019) Household and family projections, Australia. Available at www.abs.gov.au/statistics/people/population/household-and-family-projections-australia/latest-release (accessed July 2021).

Australian Institute of Health and Welfare (2020) Suicide and intentional self-harm. Available at www.aihw.gov.au/reports/australias-health/suicide-and-intentional-self-harm (accessed July 2021).

Balter, L. (2000) *Parenthood in America: An Encyclopedia*, Vol. 1, A–M. Santa Barbra, CA: ABC CLIO.

Breeders (TV Series) (2020) London: Avalon Television.

Brummelman, E., Thomaes, S., Orobio de Castro, B., Overbeek, G., and Bushman, B. (2014) "That's not just beautiful – that's incredibly beautiful!": The adverse impact of inflated praise on children with low self-esteem. *Psychological Science*, 25(3). https://doi.org/10.1177/0956797613514.

Charney, D., and Southwick, S. (2012) *Resilience: The Science of Mastering Life's Greatest Challenges*. New York: Cambridge University Press.

DiSalvo, D. (2017) 8 reasons why it's so hard to really change your behavior: Long-term behavior change is one of the hardest challenges we'll ever face. *Psychology Today*. Available at www.psychologytoday.com/us/blog/neuronarrative/201707/8-reasons-why-its-so-hard-really-change-your-behavior (accessed July 2021).

Doucleff, M., and Greenhalgh, J. (2019) The other side of anger: How Inuit parents teach kids to control their anger. Available at www.npr.org/sections/goatsandsoda/2019/03/13/685533353/a-playful-way-to-teach-kids-to-control-their-anger (accessed July 2021).

Firestone, L. (2015) How your attachment style affects your parenting. Available at www.psychologytoday.com/us/blog/compassion-matters/201510/how-your-attachment-style-affects-your-parenting (accessed July 2021).

Goleman, D. (1996) *Emotional Intelligence: Why It Can Matter More than IQ*. London: Bloomsbury.

Halford, K. (2018) How will my divorce affect my kids? Available at https://habs.uq.edu.au/article/2018/09/how-will-my-divorce-affect-my-kids (accessed July 2021).

Hand, K., Baxter, J., Carroll, M., and Budinski, M. (2020) Families in Australia survey: Life during COVID-19. Australian Institute of Family Studies. Report no. 1: Early findings. Available at https://aifs.gov.au/publications/families-australia-survey-life-during-covid-19 (accessed February 2022).

Hattie, J. (2009) *Visible Learning: A Synthesis of over 800 Meta-Analyses Relating to Achievement*. New York: Routledge.

Headspace (2021) Understanding sexuality and sexual identity. Available at https://headspace.org.au/young-people/understanding-sexuality-and-sexual-identity/ (accessed July 2021).

Hermant, N. (2017) Does helicopter parenting make kids more anxious? Available at www.abc.net.au/news/2017-11-30/new-study-draws-link-between-parenting-and-anxiety/9200940 (accessed July 2021).

Holt-Lunstad, J., Robles, T., and Sbarra, D. (2017) Advancing social connection as a public health priority in the United States. *American Psychologist*, 72(6), 517–530. Available at https://psycnet.apa.org/doiLanding?doi=10.1037%2Famp0000103 (accessed February 2022).

Jinpa, T. (2015) *A Fearless Heart: How the Courage to Be Compassionate Can Transform Our Lives*. New York: Random House.

Kurzgesagt (2019) Loneliness. Available at www.youtube.com/watch?v=n3Xv_g3g-mA&t=328s (accessed September 2022).

Le Messurier, M. (2020) *Teaching Values of Being Human*. London: Routledge.

Lillico, I. (2021) Boys Forward Institute. Available at www.boysforward.com.au (accessed July 2021).

McLeod, S. (2020) Piaget's theory and stages of cognitive development in developmental psychology. Available at www.simplypsychology.org/piaget.html (accessed July 2021).

Psynso (2021) Token economy. Available at https://psynso.com/token-economy/ (accessed July 2021).

Sanvictores, T., and Mendez, M. (2021) Types of parenting styles and effects on children. Available at www.ncbi.nlm.nih.gov/books/NBK568743/ (accessed January 2022).

Siegel, D. (2012) Dr Daniel Siegel presenting a hand model of the brain. *FtMyersFamPsych*. Available at www.youtube.com/watch?v=gm9CIJ74Oxw (accessed September 2022).

Smith, K. (2021) PTSD in children and adolescents. Available at www.psycom.net/ptsd-in-children-and-adolescents (accessed July 2021).

Swan, N. (2020) *So You Think You Know What's Good for You?* Sydney: Hachette.

The South Australian Commissioner for Children and Young People (2021) South Australia's progress on recommendations made by the UN Committee on the Rights of the Child. Child Rights Progress Reports. Available at www.ccyp.com.au/wp-content/uploads/2022/01/Child-Rights-Progress-Reports-2021.pdf (accessed January 2022).

Wachtel, T., and McCold, P. (2001) Restorative justice in everyday life. In: Strang, H. and Braithwaite, J. (eds) *Restorative Justice and Civil Society*. Cambridge: Cambridge University Press.

For Product Safety Concerns and Information please contact our EU
representative GPSR@taylorandfrancis.com
Taylor & Francis Verlag GmbH, Kaufingerstraße 24, 80331 München, Germany

www.ingramcontent.com/pod-product-compliance
Lightning Source LLC
Chambersburg PA
CBHW070343270326
41926CB00017B/3964